Student Manual to Accompany
Strategies for Counseling with Children and Their Parents

Geraldine Leitl Orton
Gannon University

Brooks/Cole Publishing Company

I⊕P® An International Thomson Publishing Company

Pacific Grove • Albany • Belmont • Bonn • Boston • Cincinnati • Detroit • Johannesburg • London
Madrid • Melbourne • Mexico City • New York • Paris • Singapore • Tokyo • Toronto • Washington

 A CLAIREMONT BOOK

Sponsoring Editor: Eileen Murphy
Editorial Assistant: Lisa Blanton
Production Coordinator: Dorothy Bell

Cover Design: E. Kelly Shoemaker
Cover Illustration: Carrie Venable
Printing and Binding: Patterson Printing

For more information, contact:

BROOKS/COLE PUBLISHING COMPANY
511 Forest Lodge Rd.
Pacific Grove, CA 93950
USA

International Thomson Publishing Europe
Berkshire House 168-173
High Holborn
London WC1V 7AA
England

Thomas Nelson Australia
102 Dodds Street
South Melbourne, 3205
Victoria, Australia

Nelson Canada
1120 Birchmount Road
Scarborough, Ontario
Canada M1K 5G4

International Thomson Editores
Seneca 53
Col. Polanco
11560 México, D.F., México

International Thomson Publishing GmbH
Königswinterer Strasse 418
53227 Bonn
Germany

International Thomson Publishing Asia
221 Henderson Road
#05-10 Henderson Building
Singapore 0315

International Thomson Publishing Japan
Hirakawacho Kyowa Building, 3F
2-2-1 Hirakawacho
Chiyoda-ku, Tokyo 102
Japan

Printed in the United States of America

10 9 8 7 6 5 4 3 2 1

ISBN 0-534-34566-2

Preface

This manual is designed to help you to learn the textbook material by providing a way to review key concepts and summarize chapter content. In combination with the text, it is intended to help you to analyze the material presented from your own counseling perspective and to develop and/or reaffirm those skills and attitudes that are appropriate for the counseling of children. It is hoped that the exercises and practical applications pique your interest, motivate you to read and research the topics you are drawn to, increase your awareness of yourself as a unique and valuable person, and enable you to integrate this self-understanding into the process of becoming a professional counselor.

Toward accomplishing these ends, each chapter of the manual includes several component parts that are organized consecutively throughout. These include: chapter summary; learning objectives; review exercises; awareness exercises; practical applications and media suggestions.

Chapter Summary

The introductory paragraph for each chapter is a brief summary and orientation to chapter content. This summary helps you focus on the topics and concepts that are featured in the chapter.

Learning Objectives

These statements are written in a "learning objective" list to show you what you can expect to learn in the chapter. These objectives are aligned with the chapter outline and chapter headings so that related content can be easily located.

Review Exercises

The questions or inquiry statements included in this section pinpoint key concepts and help you organize and remember important information by reviewing, repeating, and recalling it. Your instructor also may use this section for testing purposes or may assign these exercises as an out-of-class activity.

Awareness Exercises

The exercises in this section are intended for journaling. You should set aside a notebook specifically for responding to the statements in writing. The journal is your own private collection of self-awareness essays. In addition, your instructor may use some of the exercises for group discussion. The content of your writing may, at times, strike a sensitive chord with you. When these responses give rise to uneasy feelings, you are encouraged to discuss them with your instructor. These exercises are intended not for self-analysis or psychoanalysis but for self-understanding.

Practical Applications

The cases and examples presented in this section provide you with the opportunity to apply chapter content and practice counseling skills. Your instructor will guide you through the cases and help you to interpret, analyze and respond appropriately. The cases and examples presented are composites of actual cases encountered in professional counseling reproduced with client permission.

Media Suggestions

The books and videos listed in this section, including the inventories in Chapter 4, are additional sources of information related to the topics presented in the chapter. Many of the selections are designed to enhance the knowledge and skills of practitioners and students in counseling, social work, psychology, and education, whereas others are suggested for reading or viewing by children and parents. Each type of medium has been reviewed and is recommended for its particular suitability and relevance to chapter content. Your instructor may use some of the video suggestions for viewing as a class or may assign the study of particular books or videos as individual or group projects.

As you already know, students learn in different ways according to their personalities, interests, and particular competencies and methods of processing information. Many students find that learning material by using different faculties such as thinking, writing, and observing helps them to internalize textbook content and integrate the knowledge into their own mental arsenal. This manual, then, is intended to offer various ways of learning the material, of thinking about it, of questioning it, and of applying it. Along with the text, classroom lectures, and discussion, the manual is yet another way for you to put on your scuba gear, dive beneath the surface, and deepen your understanding, enjoyment, and appreciation for all of the new ideas, insights, and mysteries you will encounter.

Acknowledgments

It is with sincere appreciation that I wish to acknowledge those individuals who have generously given their time and talents to this effort. Special thanks goes to my colleague and dearest friend, Mary Ann Frew, not only for her contributions to the learning objectives, journal and awareness exercises but also for her expertise and unwavering support of the entire project.

A special debt of gratitude is owed to Elizabeth Akers, who read pages of manuscript, checked references, and made countless trips to the library to compile the titles for the Media Suggestions. This section also could not have been completed without the help of John Pennsy of the Gannon University library, who ordered hundreds of books through the inner-library loan; and to Helen Bolton, outreach librarian at Prendergast Library in Jamestown, NY, who recommended and reviewed many of the selections.

A big "thank you " is extended to the many students who contributed to this manual. I would especially like to acknowledge Barbara Blair, Aimee Henry, Wendy Holben, Therese McCullough, Jennifer Olszewski, Virginia Sheirer, and Christine Sullivan. Special affection and heartfelt appreciation is reserved for all the children and their parents who shared their stories and gave me permission to use them.

Finally, my deepest appreciation is extended to my family for their immeasurable love and sustained support throughout this entire effort.

Contents

Chapter 1
Growing Up in the 21st Century

This chapter provides the contextual background for understanding and applying the strategies presented in the text. An awareness of who the child and family are, against the backdrop of contemporary society, is an essential precursor to counseling. The topics and the corresponding statistics included in this chapter confront the realities characterizing the American family.

Learning Objectives

Upon completion of this chapter, you will be able to:

1. List and describe the various types of family structures represented in contemporary society.

2. Identify the "faces of poverty."

3. Outline the intervention, support, and prevention programs and discuss their relevance to counseling strategies.

Review Exercises

1. Explain why, according to the National Research Council's report in *Losing Generations: Adolescents in High Risk Settings*, seven million children and youth (between the ages of 10 and 17) are "growing up in circumstances that limit their development, compromise their health, impair their sense of self, and thereby restrict their futures."

2. According to Marian Wright Edelman, what are the four projections likely to characterize the 21st century?

3. How have families changed over the last 35 years?

4. Describe how "mothers working outside the home" have specifically affected the American family.

5. List and describe the four kinds of family structures represented in today's families.

6. How does poverty and inequality in society impact the lives of children?

7. Identify and describe the three preventive measures discussed in this chapter in which human services professionals can participate.

Awareness Exercises

1. Read the Figures 1.1 through 1.3 which are statistical portraits related to topics presented in the chapter. What is your reaction? How do you feel?

2. In your opinion, is the "family" changing or declining?

3. What type of family structure did you grow up in? What feelings do you have about it?

4. What topic or statements in this chapter do you most identify with? What, in particular, captured your attention? Why?

5. Do you disagree with any statement? Elaborate.

6. What impact, if any, do you think you can have as a human services professional in making the world a better place for children?

Practical Applications

"The Bully of the Block": The Case of Jarrod D.

Jarrod is 8-years old and was brought for counseling by his mother because of his unmanageable behavior at home. Jarrod's mother's main concern is his aggressiveness toward others at home and at school. When Jarrod is angry, which is most of the time, he hits people and makes verbal threats of aggression. Lately, he has been associating with the neighborhood toughs and staying out late. Sometimes he does not come home until nearly midnight. His mother is deeply concerned and says that she "can't make him mind." The neighbors describe Jarrod as the "bully of the block."

Jarrod is currently living with his mother and older brother Josh, age 10. His parents have been divorced since Jarrod was 5. Jarrod's father is an alcoholic, and during the years that he lived with the family, he often hit his wife and children. Since the divorce, Mr. D. has been arrested twice for beating his wife. On both occasions, Mr. D. was intoxicated and his wife required medical treatment. The children witnessed the abuse. Despite this, Jarrod wants his father to move back in with the family because he thinks his father will change. Unlike his older brother, Jarrod feels sorry for his Dad.

His teachers think that Jarrod is very bright and his intelligence scores are in the above-average range. However, his academic performance is barely passing. Jarrod's behavior in school is very disruptive. He often engages in physical fights at school and spends half of his day in the principal's office.

1. What behaviors of Jarrod's concern you? Why?

_____

_____

_____

2. What are some of the factors that are influencing Jarrod's behavior?

_____

_____

_____

3. Do you agree with Jarrod that his father will change? Explain your answer.

_____

_____

_____

4. What additional information do you need to help Jarrod?

_____

_____

_____

5. What interventions would you recommend at home, at school, and in the community?

_____

_____

_____

Media Suggestions

Books

America's Children. (1991). San Diego, CA: Greenhaven Press.

Opposing viewpoints on a number of topics that relate to America's children are presented. Noted authors debate some of the nation's most pressing problems in chapters on: What Education Policies Would Help Children? How Can Children Be Protected from Abuse? What Government Policies Would Help American's Poor Children? How Can the Health of America's Children Be Improved? Are Working Parents Harming America's Children?

Bass, D.S. (1990). *Caring Families: Supports and Interventions.* Annapolis, MD: National Association Social Workers Press.

The author identifies the stress factors and rewards that affect families and presents techniques to help the professional support them. Chapters that are especially relevant to children include: State Maternal and Child Health Programs, Temporary Child Care for Handicapped Children, and Crisis Nurseries and Department of Defense Family Support Programs.

Bass D.S. (1992). *Helping Vulnerable Youths: Runaway and Homeless Adolescents in the United States.* Annapolis, MD: National Association of Social Workers Press.

This book addressed the problems of the almost 2 million runaway and homeless adolescents and what human service professionals can do to help them. *Helping Vulnerable Youths* reports on an intensive, year-long investigation undertaken by NASW with support from the Family and Youth Services Bureau, U.S. Department of Health and Human Services.

Blankenhorn, D. (1995). *Fatherless America: Confronting Our Most Urgent Social Problem.* New York: Basic Books.

Blankenhorn's thesis is that fatherlessness is the most dangerous social trend of our generation because it weakens families, harms children, and causes or aggravates our worst social problems. In making his argument, the author contrasts the role of the "traditional" father with the "new" father and offers a controversial analysis of five categories of "almost fathers." This book provides fuel for the debate over what can be done about the decline of fatherhood in America.

Fassler, D. (1988). *Changing Families: Kids and Grownups.* Burlington, VT: Waterfront Books.

This book is intended for use by children with the assistance of parents, teachers, counselors and others. It introduces issues, expresses concerns, and addresses questions children have concerning divorce. This book is a great way to open lines of communication about this difficult topic.

Videos

Being a Single Parent.   FH: Films for the Humanities and Sciences, P.O. Box 2053, Princeton, NJ 08543-2053

This program focuses on three very different kinds of single parents: a divorced woman, an unmarried woman who chose to be a single parent, and a man who raised his two sons. The film profiles these different single-parent families and shows how each parent copes with their roles as parents and wage earners. It also discusses the psychological effects of divorce on the child. (19 minutes, color)

Can't Slow Down. FH: Films for the Humanities and Sciences, P.O. Box 2053, Princeton, NJ 08543-2053.

This film details Americans' increasingly hurried lifestyle. Americans are currently working 160 hours a year more than they did in 1970. This video points out that the reason for this increase in work can be explained by the urge to acquire, the pressure to achieve or be fired, the need to achieve outside the home, and longer commutes to work. Viewers are asked to assess how this constant rush is affecting our relationships and our health.

Children of Poverty.   FH: Films for the Humanities and Sciences, P.O. Box 2053, Princeton, NJ 08543-2053.

In America, staggering numbers of children are living in poverty. This film profiles some of these children, all in homes headed by women, and shows the effects of poverty on the children and their mothers. (26 minutes, color)

Families First. FH: Films for the Humanities and Sciences, P.O. Box 2053, Princeton, NJ 08543-2053.

This video features an approach known as "family preservation services" (FPS). In the program, case workers visit families who are experiencing personal crises that threaten them with the loss of their children to foster care. The stories of these families, and the caseworkers who help them learn the skills that they need to stay together, highlight a positive approach to coping with one of society's most distressing problems. (90 minutes, color)

Families Matter. FH: Films for the Humanities and Sciences, P.O. Box 2053, Princeton, NJ 08543-2053.

This film examines some of society's negative impacts on families and children and explores ways to rebuild support for American families. A number of experts including Richard Louv, author of *Childhood's Future*, discuss ways to create a more supportive social climate for families. (60 minutes, color)

Family in Crisis. FH: Films for the Humanities and Sciences, P.O. Box 2053, Princeton, NJ 08543-2053.

This film, adapted from a Phil Donahue program, centers on the plight of poor children growing up in single-parent households. It examines the problems facing children who are growing up without fathers and the cycle of poverty that especially affects minority families. (28 minutes, color)

Fatherless in America. FH: Films for the Humanities and Sciences, P.O. Box 2053, Princeton, NJ 08543-2053

This video highlights the fact that nearly 40% of American children sleep in homes where their father does not live. It discusses the problem, its causes, and its effects, from poverty to violence. Efforts to reverse the growing trend toward fatherlessness in America are also addressed. (26 minutes, color)

Kids Out of Control. FH: Films for the Humanities and Sciences, P.O. Box 2053, Princeton, NJ 08543-2053.

This video presents a number of all-too-common scenarios: the eighth-grader whose drug use has completely altered his personality; a young girl who became severely depressed because of work, school, and family pressures; and a teenage rape victim who ran away from home, attempted suicide. and became addicted to drugs. The film helps others determine whether a child is in need of help and offers an inside look at a group therapy session.

Kids Raising Kids: The Education of a Teen Mother. FH: Films for the Humanities and Sciences, P.O. Box 2053, Princeton, NJ 08543-2053.

This film features two teenage mothers who are able to complete their high school education because of a high school day care program. The advantages of accepting teenage mothers and fathers in the high school education system are also highlighted. (24 minutes, color)

Latchkey Families. FH: Films for the Humanities and Sciences, P.O. Box 2053, Princeton, NJ 08543-2053.

This program offers specific help to working parents with children who are on their own after school. Education and law enforcement specialists explain how parents can provide for the physical safety and emotional needs of their children. Guidelines for setting rules and assigning chores are discussed as efforts to help children toward maturity and independence.

On Values: The Family. FH: Films for the Humanities and Sciences, P.O. Box 2053, Princeton, NJ 08543-2053

The changing structure of families in America today and the consequences for our children are examined in this hour long presentation. Barbara Defoe Whitehead, social historian and vice president of the Institute of American Values, is featured along with several noted authors on the subject of families and children. (60 minutes, color)

Running Out of Time: Time Pressure, Overtime, and Overwork. FH: Films for the
Humanities and Sciences, P.O. Box 2053, Princeton, NJ 08543-2053.

The impact of time pressure and overwork on American society is explored. This
video addresses how much activity people fit into their busy lives, how much
responsibility they increasingly assume and how little time remains for leisure. (52
minutes, color)

Society's Problems in Children's Lives. FH: Films for the Humanities and Sciences, P.O.
Box 2053, Princeton, NJ 08543-2053.

This program explores the many societal problems facing children today including
drugs, crime, teenage pregnancy, rising school dropout rates, lack of educational
opportunities, the changing family, and the possible reduction in welfare benefits. These
problems and their impact on the quality of children's lives are discussed. (28 minutes,
color)

T. Berry Brazelton: The Changing Family and Its Implications. FH: Films for the
Humanities and Sciences, P.O. Box 2053, Princeton, NJ 08543-2053

The author of a number of books on childraising takes this opportunity to discuss
the problems and challenges of working parents. (50 minutes, color)

Chapter Two
The Developing Child

The content of this chapter provides the framework for counseling that applies to the entire text. A chronicle of familial, social, economic, and political forces that have shaped children's lives for centuries is presented and analyzed. In addition, an overview of the development of healthy children from birth to age 12 is included. Specifically, this discussion includes developmental milestones: gross and fine motor movement; language acquisition; imagination, humor, and play behaviors; cognitive or thinking skills; emotional development; and social interaction. With emphasis on child development related to pre-schoolers and school age children, this chapter is intended to reinforce the concepts presented in child development courses. In addition, the common developmental problems encountered by healthy children are discussed, and guidelines for referral are presented.

Learning Objectives

Upon completing this chapter, you will be able to:

1. Identify important influences on the child's development.

2. List age-related landmarks in motor, cognitive, psychosocial, language, and emotional development.

3. Identify and discuss the contributions of major child development theorists.

4. Describe the common developmental problems of healthy children.

5. List and explain the guidelines for referring a child to counseling that can be utilized by parents, teachers, and clinicians.

Review Exercises

1. What influences from the past (Middle Ages to the present) regarding attitudes toward children are significant in the development of society's contemporary view of how children should be treated?

2. How do the family and social institutions impact child development?

3. List the landmarks in motor development for children age 2 to 6.

4. Define and describe Piaget's "sensorimotor period."

5. Define object permanence. When does it begin?

6. Summarize communication methods from birth to age 2.

7. List and describe Erikson's stages of psychosocial development that apply to children and adolescents.

8. Summarize language, play, cognitive, emotional, and social development in preschoolers.

9. Summarize motor, language, cognitive, and emotional, and social development in school-age children.

10. Discuss the positive and negative influences on development of the following: dependency and attachment; anger and aggression; jealousy and rivalry; fear and anxiety.

11. Define the following terms: *shyness, coy response, embarrassment; worry, anxiety; anger, hostile aggression, instrumental aggression, uncontrolled aggression, and submissiveness; jealousy, and sibling rivalry.*

12. List and explain the six questions used to determine whether a child is experiencing a normal behavior problem or one that requires counseling.

Awareness Exercises

1. What is the significance (as related to chapter content) of the poem included at the beginning of this chapter? What is your reaction to the poem?

2. Do you think some of the attitudes presented in the historical perspective of Childhood Through the Ages exist in contemporary society? Support your opinions with examples.

3. When you read the ages and stages of normal development, can you identify with them? Do you think your own development was thwarted in any way? Why? How?

4. Do you recall any riddles and/or chants that were favorites of yours in childhood? In retrospect, what purpose do you think they served?

5. Did you have friends in your preadolescent school years? Explain or elaborate your answer. If you did have one or more friends, what do you most remember about them or the things that you did together?

6. When you read the common developmental problems of healthy children, do you remember having any of these problems as a child? Have parents or others ever alluded to any of the developmental issues listed in review question 10? For example, has anyone said to you: " You were really shy as a child"? What impact do you think these issues might have had on your development as an adult?

Practical Applications

"Always on the Fence": The Case of Marta O.

Marta is 9 years old and is in the fourth grade. Her peers notice that she is "always on the fence" and can never make a decision. She seems to wait and follow others. She asks her mother constantly, "What should I do?" Marta's mother complains that Marta doesn't act like a 9-year-old and is not able to do a lot of things that her older sister did at the same age.

At school, Marta is getting good grades but requires a lot of help and reassurance from her teachers. Socially, she has few friends and seems to prefer the company of older people, particularly her older sister (age 13) and her mother. Marta tells her mother that the other children don't like her, and she doesn't want to go to school most of the time. On the playground, Marta likes to stand near the teacher. She has always been taught what is right, and when she sees the kids doing things that she considers wrong, she tells the teacher.

Mrs. O. complained to the counselor that "I am 'doing' for Marta what she should be doing for herself." Mrs. O. notices that Marta can never make up her mind but claims that Marta is just like Mrs. O's mother, who could never make a decision either.

Marta's mother wants to help her. She feels that Marta is lonely and picked on by the other children. She buys Marta nice things and tells her "not to pay any attention to the other kids because they probably aren't nice anyway." Some days, Mrs. O. feels sorry for Marta and lets her skip school. Mrs. O. hopes that Marta will outgrow this stage.

1. Identify some of the behaviors that concern you in this case. What do these behaviors suggest?

_____

_____

_____

2. What are some factors that might be contributing to Marta's behavior?

_____

_____

_____

3. Do you think that Marta's behavior warrants a referral? Why or why not?

_____

_____

_____

4. What do you think could be done to help Marta become a happier child?

_____

_____

_____

"A Perfect Little Lady": The Case of SooLing

SooLing is 6 years old and is in the first grade. Her mother and father, ages 50 and 56 respectively, were thrilled with their menopausal baby, lavishing much attention on their only child. They describe her as "absolutely no problem." They are proud of the fact that SooLing is fastidious; always cleaning and straightening. She is physically healthy, of average intelligence and as her father describes her "a perfect little lady."

At school, SooLing's teacher has observed her behavior since school started three months ago and is deeply concerned. SooLing has no friends and seeks to seclude herself from the other children. The teacher asked two girls in the class to join SooLing for lunch. They did so but later complained that SooLing was " no fun," corrected their manners constantly, and folded all the lunch trash into neat little piles.

Her parents have asked school officials to excuse SooLing from gym and art classes because all the activity and turmoil is too much for her. The officials have refused, and SooLing has become noticeably tense on activity day and often ends up on the nurse's cot with a headache or stomachache.

SooLing's parents have never left her with a baby-sitter, and they usually take her with them when they go out. She dines in restaurants with her parents and often accompanies them to the ballet and to the symphony. Her mother and father are delighted that she is so well behaved. They would not dream of letting her play with other children because they would not be "on her level." Consequently, SooLing does not play with the children who live in her neighborhood. Her parents' friends are older and do not have children her age. Therefore, her only contact with other children is at school.

1. What are some of SooLing's behaviors that concern you? Why?

_____

_____

_____

2. Are SooLing's behaviors appropriate for her age and developmental level?

_____

_____

_____

3. Do you think that SooLing's behaviors warrant a referral?

_____

_____

_____

4. What additional information would you need to make a referral? Use the guidelines for referral to make your determination.

_____

_____

_____

GUIDELINES FOR REFERRAL

These questions follow established assessment criteria related to appropriateness, frequency, duration, course, intensity and impairment. Using the case of SooLing, fill in the answers to each question and decide whether this case warrants referral to a mental health professional.

1. Is the child's behavior appropriate for his or her age and developmental level?

Allowing for individual differences and for developmental lags, consider whether the child is able to manage the appropriate developmental tasks for his or her particular age range (e.g., early, middle, and later childhood).

_____

_____

_____

_____

2. Is the child's behavior appropriate considering the circumstances? Is the child's behavior an expected reaction to the situation? For example, what if a child, embarrassed by the peer group, blushes? What if a provoked child fights back? Are these normal responses? What about the unexpected reactions? Sometimes a child overreacts, underreacts, or doesn't react at all. These unexpected reactions give clues to the child's stability.

_____

_____

_____

_____

3.   **How frequently   does the child display the problem   behavior?**   Because development is not a smooth progression and children often regress or slip back to behaviors that were characteristic of a previous level, counselors, parents and teachers need to be aware of how often the child has this problem.

_____

_____

_____

_____

4.   **What is the duration of the problem?**   Determining how long the problem has lasted will help the parent, teacher, or counselor decide whether a referral is necessary. Many developmental problems seem to disappear as quickly as they came.   Specific fears are a good example of a normal developmental problem.

_____

_____

_____

_____

5. **Has there been a sudden change in the child's behavior?** It is important to determine whether the behavior that concerns the parent, teacher, or counselor is a sudden departure from the pattern of behavior that the child has been exhibiting previously. If so, the counselor or therapist must look to the child's immediate environment to see what might be causing this sudden change. Sometimes sudden changes of behavior are indicative of abuse or family disruptions caused by death, divorce, or domestic violence.

_____

_____

_____

_____

6. **Is the behavior interfering with the child's overall functioning?** Is the child suffering somehow as a result of the problem? If so, to what degree is the child's functioning affected? Is the behavior causing the child to be rejected by agemates; preventing the child from benefitting from school instruction; blocking the healthy expression of emotion, or interfering with the child's happiness? Perhaps the behavior is affecting only one area of the child's development; perhaps it is affecting all areas.

_____

_____

_____

_____

Media Suggestions

Books

Craig, G.J. & Kermis, M.D. (1995). *Children Today.* Upper Saddle River, NJ:
    Prentice-Hall.

This book explores the biological, physical, cognitive, social, and emotional development of children. It offers an open-ended perspective and includes new research, different and opposing views, applications to real life situations, and cross-cultural issues.

Flavell, J.H., Miller, P.H. & Miller, S.A. (1993). *Cognitive Development* (3rd. ed.).
    Odessa, FL: Psychological Assessment Resources.

This introductory text deals with pertinent topics in the field of childhood cognitive development. It highlights the intellectual growth of children in infancy, early childhood, middle childhood, and adolescence.

Harris, R.H. & Liebert, R.M. (1991). *The Child: A Contemporary View of Development.*
    Upper Saddle River, NJ: Prentice Hall.

In this text, which combines a "journalistic" style of writing with a scholarly approach to data and theory, children are viewed as playing an active role in their own development.

Hughes, F.P., Noppe, L.D. & Noppe, I.C. (1996). *Child Development.* Upper Saddle
    River, NJ: Prentice-Hall.

This text feature a chapter on some of the problems (i.e., Attention Deficit Hyperactivity Disorder) that can interfere with healthy development. It also includes extensive coverage on how play both reflects and facilitates child development.

Kersey, K. (1986). *Helping Your Child Handle Stress.* Washington, D.C:
    Acropolis Books.
This book offers parents a guide to both the normal and abnormal stresses of childhood today. Parents learn strategies for helping their children through the pitfalls of growing up in a confusing time.

Inventories

Hresko, W.P., Miguel, S.A., Sherbenou, R.J. & Burton, S.D. (1994). *Developmental Observation Checklist System: A Systems Approach to Assessing Very Young Children.*   Austin, TX: Pro-Ed.

The DOCS is a three-part system for the assessment of very young children with respect to general development (DC), adjustment behavior (ABC), and parent stress and support (PSSC). It is suitable for birth through age 6 and can be completed by parents or caregivers.

Videos

Breaking the Unseen Barrier: Self-Concept and Social Skills (1989). Insight Media, 2162 Broadway, New York, NY 10024.

This video emphasizes how some children with academic disabilities suffer from poor self-concept and social skills. It illustrates how teachers can work together with parents to help children improve their self-esteem.

Cognitive Development.   FH: Films for the Humanities and Sciences, P.O. Box 2053, Princeton, NJ 08543-2053.

Piaget's theory is examined and critically evaluated in light of current research. Each stage of cognitive development from birth to age 12 is illustrated with examples of children's behavior at each level.   The program concludes that children are more cognitively capable at an earlier age than Piaget suggested , but it is the ages rather than the stages that are disputed. (60 minutes, color)

How Relationships Are Formed. Films for the Humanities and Sciences, P.O. Box 2053, Princeton, NJ 08543-2053.

This film focuses on the infant's needs for stimulation and love. Regardless of the culture, babies around the world understand the smile as a signal of recognition and pleasure. (24 minutes, color)

Language Development FH: Films for the Humanities and Sciences, P.O. Box
2053, Princeton, NJ 08543-2053.

This film emphasizes the development of language in babies and young children. The arguments for and against the nature-nurture debate and the interactionist view are featured. (40 minutes, color)

Pressure-Cooked Kids. FH: Films for the Humanities and Sciences, P.O. Box
2053, Princeton, NJ 08543-2053.

What can be done to prepare teenagers to balance the pressures of home and the workplace? This film talks about the problems associated with stress and discusses ways to teach young people how they can cope with it as adults. (28 minutes, color)

Promoting Wholesome Sibling Relationships. (1990). Insight Media, 2162
Broadway, New York, NY 10024.

The underlying motives for sibling rivalry are investigated in this video. It examines ways in which competition and rivalry can be a positive experience and provides four steps for effectively handling sibling rivalry. (10 minutes)

Self-Esteem in School-Age Children.(1990). Insight Media, 2162 Broadway, New
York, NY 10024.

The video explores the components of the self, including self-concept (cognitive awareness of personal attributes), self-control (behavioral conduct) and self-esteem (feelings of worth). It explores how adults can enhance a child's self-esteem. (25 minutes)

Self-Esteem and How We Learn. (1992). Insight Media, 2162 Broadway, New York,
NY. 10024.

Focusing on school-age children, this video examines how self-esteem affects personal satisfaction and academic success. It illustrates how a positive self-image decreases the likelihood of teen pregnancy and involvement in drugs and crime. (30 minutes).

The Development of Self. FH: Films for the Humanities and Sciences, P.O. Box
2053, Princeton, NJ 08543-2053.

In the first year of life, the child develops mobility and the ability to send and receive psychological messages. How the child learns to deal with the social world around it is the subject of this video. (23 minutes, color)

The Influence of the Family: On the Home Front (1991). Insight Media, 2162
Broadway, New York, NY 10024.

The effects of complex family interactions on the developing child are explored. This program examines how different family structures, (e.g. dual income, single-parent, and reconstituted) affect children. Discipline and parental control tactics are explored as well as how birth order and age span affect sibling rivalry.

Chapter 3
The Vulnerable Child

The nature, character, and substance of the "vulnerable child" is explored in this chapter. Each categorization of vulnerability is described, and counseling strategies are identified and applied. The role of the counselor as a significant resource for assisting children on the road to healthy development emerges in this chapter. Support services for children and parents are included.

Learning Objectives

Upon completion of this chapter, you will be able to:

1. Define and describe child abuse and neglect.

2. Describe the characteristics of children who have been victims of abuse, are parented by an alcoholic, were impacted by divorce or AIDS, or are in mourning.

3. Choose and apply counseling strategies appropriate for each characterization of the vulnerable child.

4. List support groups available for children and parents who are in the situations depicted in this chapter.

Review Exercises

1. Define child abuse and describe its scope.

2. What are the characteristics of the abusive parent?

3. Differentiate between the various types of abuse and neglect.

4. Identify and describe the counseling strategies related to the counseling of abused children.

5. Describe the characteristics of a child of an alcoholic.

6. Identify and describe the counseling strategies recommended for children of alcoholics.

7. What is the impact of divorce and blended families on the development of children?

8. What are the psychological tasks associated with divorce?

9. Identify and describe the counseling strategies related to counseling of children of divorce.

10. Explain the impact of AIDS on children and their families.

11. Identify and describe the counseling strategies related to the counseling of children with AIDS.

12. What are the contributing influences related to how a child copes with death?

13. Identify and describe the counseling strategies related to the counseling of children in mourning.

14. List the support services that might be recommended to parents of children with the vulnerabilities discussed in this chapter.

Awareness Exercises

1. What are your feelings related to child abuse? What is your attitude toward parents and others who physically, emotionally, or sexually abuse children?

2. Have you ever known an alcoholic? What was the emotional, financial and other personal cost to him-or herself and the family?

3. What is your view of divorce and what are your personal feelings about the impact of divorce on children?

4. What fears do you have regarding AIDS or your ability or willingness to counsel children with AIDS?

5. Did someone close to you die when you were a child or adolescent? What were your feelings? How do you feel now about what you were told about death and how the adults around you coped with the loss?

6. Do you think you would feel uncomfortable using any of the counseling strategies described in this chapter? State your reasons.

Practical Applications

"The War of the Rosens": The Case of Joel R.

Mr. and Mrs. Rosen argue constantly. On numerous occasions, Mrs. Rosen has left her husband and three sons, Warren (age 10), Joel (age 6), and Jacob (age 4), but she always returns in a week or two. Joel, who appears to be the most affected by his mother's frequent absences, cries and screams each time his mother leaves. His older half-brother, Warren, tries to comfort him and says, " Don't worry Joel, she'll come back; she always does."

Recently, Mr. Rosen decided that enough is enough! He has issued an ultimatum to his wife: "You can either stay and try to work out our problems or you can leave and let the family recover from the damages." Mrs. Rosen has decided to move out for good. She wants to take Warren, her son by a previous marriage, with her but he wants no part of that arrangement. He wants to stay with his adoptive father and his half-brothers, Joel and Jacob.

Since his mother left, Joel has been waking up in the middle of the night crying and worrying. Afraid to fall asleep, Joel is convinced that something bad is going to happen to him or his family, He does not want to be alone, and lately he has made many requests to sleep in his dad's room. Because he fears that his father might leave him too, Joel stays close and seldom lets his father out of his sight. This desire for physical proximity has prompted Joel's dad to refer to him affectionately as "my little shadow."

Joel has always been a very outgoing child who loved to play with the neighborhood children. Lately, however, he has been secluding himself and spending most of his afternoons playing video games in his room. At school, Joel refuses to play with the other children. Instead he sits at his desk and draws pictures of a family that includes a mom, a dad, and three boys.

Recently, his teachers have noted that Joel displays a wide range of behaviors which were not evident just a few months ago. On several occasions, he has been uncharacteristically aggressive toward other children during group activities, yet he frequently cries and withdraws when things are not going his way. During gym class, Joel complains of a stomachache and sits on the sidelines or goes to the nurse's office. His teachers are concerned about these sudden changes in behavior, which suggest sadness, mood swings, withdrawal and aggressiveness.

At home, Joel and his brothers are being cared for by their father's sister. At first Joel refused his aunt's small gifts and offers of help. He thought that by rejecting her, he was being loyal to his mother. To make matters worse, Joel would deliberately misbehave, and when his aunt tried to help him get back on track he would say, "I don't have to listen to you; you're not my mom!" Lately, however, Joel seems to be more attached to his Aunt Judith and has stopped giving her such a hard time.

According to the literature reviewed in the text, children express certain common reactions to separation and divorce. These reactions include: a) mourning responses such as confusion, anger, denial, depression and feelings of hopelessness; b) fear of rejection and feelings of abandonment and powerlessness; c) anger; and d) resentment and intense loneliness.

1. Based on the information given in the case, discuss some of the reactions that you think Joel is having to his parents' conflict and his mother's frequent absences.

_____

_____

_____

_____

2. Judith Wallerstein identified a number of "psychological tasks" that children who experience divorce encounter. Explain these tasks as they apply to Joel.

_____

_____

_____

_____

3. What counseling strategies do you think are needed to help Joel overcome the loss of daily contact with his mother? Who should be involved in the counseling process?

_____

_____

_____

_____

Media Suggestions

Books

Crewdson, J. (1988). *By Silence Betrayed: Sexual Abuse of Children in America.*
    Boston, MA: Little Brown.

This book is a riveting examination of one of society's most disturbing, pervasive problems. It raises touch questions and speaks with brilliant insight, compassion, and objectivity about a subject that is painful to contemplate but far too important to ignore.

Dane, E. (1990). *Painful Passages: Working with Children with Learning
    Disabilities.* Annapolis, MD: National Association of Social Workers (NASW).

Dane addresses issues such as truancy, nonattendance, family disruption, delinquency, and other problems that often plague children with learning disabilities.

Francke, L.B. (1984). *Growing Up Divorced.* New York: Fawcett.

In this authoritative handbook the author offers a complete description of the crises facing "divorced children." She focuses on relieving the distress before it becomes damage and offers comprehensive advice on how to handle even the roughest aftershocks of divorce.

Getzoff, A. (1985). *Step Kids.* New York: Walker & Co.

This is a survival guide for teenagers in stepfamilies. Among the things stepkids discuss are how to talk to a stepparent, parents' divorce, stepsiblings, sex in the stepfamily, how to hold a family council, and more.

Helmering, D. W. (1981). *I Have Two Families.* Nashville, TN: Abingdon.

Divorce isn't the end of the world. That's what children learn from this useful book. They also find out they aren't alone when they have difficult, unhappy feelings. Their feelings are shared by others and can be talked about.

Krementz, J. (1984). *How It Feels When Parents Divorce*. New York: Alfred Knopf.

Nineteen boys and girls aged 7 to 16 talk about the shock and anger, confusion and pain of divorce. Their openness in discussing these feelings will provide comfort and insight to both children and parents.

Kubler-Ross, E. (1989). *AIDS: The Ultimate Challenge*. New York: Collier Books.

Dr. Kubler-Ross, renowned for her work with the terminally ill, focuses on victims of AIDS. With compassion and insight, she gives comfort to those who are seriously ill and helps them through the critical "stages of dying."

Kurland, M. (1990). *Coping with Family Violence*. New York: Rosen Group.

This book deals with the violent confrontations that occur in otherwise ordinary appearing families. Sections include: "Battered Children," "Dad Loves Me More," and "Caught in the Crossfire." Actual cases show ways to handle problems and how and where to get help for teens.

Middleton-Moz, J. & Dwinell, L. (1986). *After the Tears: Reclaiming the Personal Losses of Childhood*. Deerfield Beach, FL: Health Communications.

Grief and loss reflect the family legacy of alcoholism. Children from these homes suffer long-term depression and erosion of their sense of self-worth. This book will tell the reader what to do. . . after the tears.

Porterfield, K.M. (1990). *Coping with an Alcoholic Parent*. New York: Rosen Group.

Over seven million children in the United States live in families where one or both parents are alcoholics. This reassuring book helps teens deal with problems and take care of themselves when things aren't right at home.

Prokop, M.S. (1986). *Divorce Happens to the Nicest Kids: A Book of Hope, Love and Understanding*. Warren, OH: Alegra House Publishing.

This self-help book is for kids aged 3 to 15 and their parents. It articulates the unspoken fears of children of divorce in a way that is honest, comforting, and supportive.

Russell, P. & Stone, B. (1986). *Do You Have a Secret? How to Get Help with Scary Secrets.* Minneapolis, MN: Compcare Publications.

> Every child faces the possibility of abuse, so every child needs to know what to do about it. Scary secrets, like being touched inappropriately, can trap children into a pattern of abuse in which they've threatened them "not to tell." Scary secrets *must* be told!   This is a book designed to be read by children or to children by adults. It includes an adult guide and sensitive illustrations.

Sanford, L.T. (1982). *Silent Children: A Parent's Guide to the Prevention of Child Sexual Abuse.* New York:McGraw-Hill.

> This guide will tell you how and what to say to your children about sexual abuse. Emphasis is placed on encouraging a strong sense of a child's legitimate rights as a human being, including the right to not accept inappropriate behavior from grown-ups.

Sweet, P. (1985). *Something Happened to Me.* Racine, WI: Mother Courage.

> A book for children and families where sexual abuse has occurred.   This sensitively handled information will help the child talk about this "forbidden" topic so expert help can begin.

Videos

An American Stepfamily. FH: Films for the Humanities and Sciences, PO Box 2053, Princeton, NJ 08543-2053

> Conflicting loyalties, rivalries, and the problems associated with dealing with former spouses and the three categories of kids-- his, hers and theirs-- are examined in this film. (26 minutes, color)

Child Abuse.   FH: Films for the Humanities and Sciences, P.O. Box 2053, Princeton, NJ 08543-2053.

> In this video, which deals with sexual and physical abuse, a clinical social worker discusses the effects of abuse on the child and explains how she helps children re-create what has happened to them. A therapist who works with sex offenders describes the common characteristics of offenders. (19 minutes, color)

Childhood Physical Abuse. FH: Films for the Humanities and Sciences, P.O. Box 2053, Princeton, NJ 08543-2053.

This video covers the range of problems associated with the physical abuse of children including: adults most likely to abuse their children, signs of abuse, effects of abuse on children, ways to deal with abuse, what happens when abuse is reported and how abusive parents can change their behavior. If and how abuse can be prevented is also discussed. (26 minutes, color)

Children of Divorce. FH: Films for the Humanities and Sciences, P.O. Box 2053, Princeton, NJ 08543-2053.

This specially-adaptedPhil Donahue program examines the effects of divorce on children. It addresses some of the pain, confusion, guilt and displacement that accompanies parental divorce. (28 minutes, color)

No More Secrets. FH: Films for the Humanities and Sciences, P.O. Box 2053, Princeton, NJ 08543-2053.

This program offers the stories of sexually abused children and of adults who were abused as children, follows the trial of an adult accused of abusing eight girls and shows how children can be encouraged to share their secret with those who can help put an end to the abuse. (24 minutes, color)

Psychological Symptoms of the Sexually Abused Child. (1993). Insight Media, 2162 Broadway, New York, NY 10024.

Viewers are taught to recognize the psychological symptoms of the sexually abused child and how to involve the foster parent, child protective-services worker, and the mental-health professional in a team approach to caring for the child. (39 minutes)

Toward An Understanding of Child Sexual Abuse. (1991). Insight Media, 2162 Broadway, New York, NY. 10024.

This video comes in a three-part series: Psychosexual Development of Children, Dynamics and Treatment. In the first part, normal sexual development is presented, and sexual abuse is defined in relation to developmental norms. In the second part, entitled Dynamics, the many categories of sexual abuse are described, the dynamics of child seduction are explored and a legal definition is given. Finally, Treatment examines all of the major treatment modalities for all parties involved. (Each part is 30 minutes)

Chapter 4
Assessment and Treatment Plan

Assessment and treatment planning are addressed in this chapter. Components discussed are the therapeutic environment and relationship; obtaining information about the child through interviews and observations, formal and informal assessment techniques; and goal planning and treatment strategies.

Learning Objectives

Upon completion of this chapter, you will be able to:

1. Recognize the characteristics of a therapeutic environment.

2. Describe a therapeutic relationship.

3. Identify and discuss assessment techniques.

4. Discuss the role of goal setting in developing the treatment plan.

5. Describe strategy and activity options related to the treatment plan.

Review Exercises

1. Characterize an ideal therapeutic environment.

2. What factors are essential in a therapeutic relationship?

3. List the five important areas of a child's life that the counselor will need to assess.

4. How can information about the child's life be gathered?

5. Differentiate between formal and informal assessment techniques.

6. Explain the purpose and process of making tentative hypotheses in treatment planning.

7. Why is goal setting an important part of treatment planning? Give examples of the kinds of goals and the related strategies, and identify who would participate in this phase of the treatment plan.

8. Identify obstacles in treatment planning that might adversely affect the counseling process.

9. How can progress in implementing the treatment plan be measured?

Awareness Exercises

1. Read the definition of counseling that precedes Chapter 4. How do you define "optimum development and well-being" ?

2. Toward the goal of increasing self-awareness, essential to the counselor in the counseling process, comment on the following:

   a. Your ability to express warmth and acceptance.

   b. Your own experience with being loved and loving unconditionally.

   c. Your ability to be empathic.

   d. Your acceptance and understanding of people of other cultures.

Practical Applications

The "Betty Crocker" of the Family: The Case of Keeva M.

Keeva M. is a 13-year-old 8th grader in an affluent suburban community. She is the only child of a CEO of a large company and his wife, who recently opened her own art gallery. Keeva has always been an ideal child, an honor student and a talented pianist. She particularly enjoys cooking and has become "the Betty Crocker" of the family.

In the past six months, much to the dismay of her parents, Keeva has lost almost forty pounds, dropping from 132 to 95 pounds. Initially in the summer, she began dieting since both she and her mother felt that she was getting a little overweight. However, when she had lost the desired 12 pounds, she still felt fat and continued to restrict her diet. She also decided to exercise and, being unhappy about the proportions of her body, did 200 sit-ups a day. Her body image seemed distorted, as she insisted that she was fat. When she was down to 110 pounds her family began to protest her dieting but she was resistant to their overtures. She became touchy in a manner that was alien to her usually cheerful disposition and avoided communicating with her mother. She drove herself through her busy high school day, persevering in homework to receive bonus points that would assure high marks. By December she was down to 92 pounds, her menstrual periods had stopped, and she appeared gaunt. Her ankles were swelling at the end of the day and a downy hair appeared on the back of her skinny arms.

Keeva's parents' pleas to resume eating were ineffective. Keeva felt that she was not too thin and that her parents were incorrect and over-concerned, and she expressed fear about becoming fat again. Her parents sought medical help, and when the family physician could find no organic reason for her weight loss, Keeva was referred to a hospital that specializes in eating disorders. A team of mental health professionals, including doctors, nurses, psychologists, counselors and social workers are helping Keeva to return to physical and emotional health.

Preliminary assessment revealed a competitive family atmosphere with tremendous pressures for success on all members. Recently Keeva's father has been out of town almost continuously and his time for Keeva, which in the past had been a weekly outing, was nonexistent. In the absence of the father, the paternal grandmother visited more frequently, ostensibly to help the family during her son's absence, but in reality she intimidated and controlled Keeva's mother. Keeva's place in the family was undefined and she regressed to a clinging relationship with her mother. The mother, too, felt herself diminished by the lack of contact with her previously loving and supportive husband and by the domination of the grandmother.

In the initial interview, Keeva stated that it seemed that she could never meet the standards of her family. She felt that she was on a treadmill and was being carried into a life that she did not want. It became apparent that as a result of this feeling, Keeva resorted to the only independent act that she was capable of-- control of her body via eating and exercise.

1. What aspects of Keeva's behavior concern you and why?

_____

_____

_____

_____

2. How would you diagnose her problem?

_____

_____

_____

_____

3. What factors may be contributing to her behavior?

_____

_____

_____

_____

4. What additional information is needed? (See the following Child Information Form for more data.)

_____

_____

_____

_____

CHILD INFORMATION FORM

IDENTIFYING INFORMATION

Child's Name   *Keeva M.*   Nickname   *None*

Date of Birth   *1-20-82*   Sex: *F*   Present Age   *13*

School Attending   *South East*   Grade   *8*   Teacher   *Ms. Friendly*

Birth Order: *1st* 2nd 3rd 4th 5th 6th of *1* 2 3 4 5 6 children

Child lives with   *Both Parents*

Name of Parents / Guardians _____   *Mr. and Mrs. M.*   _____

Address   _____   *Anywhere, USA*

Home Phone_____ Work Phone(s)_____ _____

MAJOR CONCERNS

    Please describe, in your own words, your concerns about your child and the reasons that you are seeking help.

> *Keeva refuses to eat and has lost 37 pounds in the last six months.*
> *She seems depressed and doesn't go out with her friends. She*
> *is always cold and is cranky and irritable, which isn't characteristic.*

When were these difficulties first noticed? Please explain as fully as you can.

> *She began dieting early last summer, but we didn't notice her weight loss*
> *until about December when she stopped menstruating*

Has this child had any previous professional assistance with the problems stated here? If so, please provide information

Agency/Professional   Approximate dates   What was done?

Dr. I. Care   *12-95*   *Physical exam and referral*

MEDICAL HISTORY

Please describe this child's general health.

Good-Excellent until this illness.

Has he/she had any serious illnesses, accidents, or injuries?

Broken left arm at age 3

Please give reasons and approximate dates for any hospitalizations.

None

Are there any conditions that require regular medical care?

None until recently

Does this child take any medications on a regular basis? If so, please note type of medication and frequency of use.

Dr. I. Care prescribed Prozac- 10 mg. on 12-12-95

Does the child have any difficulties with vision or hearing? Note date and results of any previous vision or hearing examinations.

None

Does the child have any allergies? If yes, please identify.

None

Pediatrician/ Family physician name. *Dr. I. Care. Anywhere, USA*

Date of last physical examination   *12-12-95*

DEVELOPMENTAL HISTORY

Please note any complications during **pregnancy** with this child (such as, illness, accidents, prolonged emotional stress, etc.). *__Planned pregnancy, no unusual circumstances__*

Delivery was on time? *__Yes__*   early_____late_____Length of labor *__15 hours__*
Any complications? *__None__*
Birth weight *__8 lbs. 15 oz.__*   Incubator? *__No__*   Need oxygen? *__No__*

How would you describe your child as an infant?   *__An easy-going, happy baby who smiled a lot.__*

Has this child had any problems with motor development (such as difficulty learning to walk, poor coordination, difficulty coloring, cutting or drawing)? *__Keena has always been ahead of her age-mates. She has good coordination and took dance lessons from age 5.__*

At what age was the child able to:
Smile and recognize people *__3 months.__*	Feed self with spoon *__10-11 months__*
Sit up without support *__8 months.__*	Drink from glass/cup *__10-11 months.__*
Stand alone *__11 months.__*	Ride a tricycle *__3 years.__*
Walk alone *__12-13 months.__*	Tie shoes *__5 years.__*

Has this child had any problems with understanding or speaking language? *__None__*

At what age (months/years and months) was this child able to:
Coo and babble *__3 months.__*	Combine two words *__18 months__*
Say first words *__1 year.__*	Follow simple directions *__2 years.__*
Name people and things *__18 months.__*	Use short sentences *__2 years.__*

Does this child have current problems with soiling or wetting during the day or at night? If so, explain. *__None__*

At what age did this child:
Begin toilet training *__22 months__*	Complete toilet training *__24 months__*
Remain dry during the day *__24 months__*	Remain dry during the night *__24 months__*

Does this child have current sleep disturbances such as difficulty falling asleep, getting up in the middle of the night or being difficult to wake?   *__No__*

LEARNING DEVELOPMENT

Compared to other children you know, this child did/does have difficulty with:

	Did	Does		Did	Does
Identifying basic colors	___	___	Telling Time	___	___
Learning the alphabet	___	___	Adding numbers	___	___
Learning to count	___	___	Subtracting	___	___
Recognizing numbers	___	___	Multiplying	___	___
Reading	___	___	Dividing	___	___
Printing	___	___	Cursive writing	___	___
Spelling correctly	___	___	Retaining information	___	___
Understanding what is read	___	___			

Please note the grades and explain the circumstances if this child has:
a) Had extended or frequent absences   *__No__*
b) Had to repeat the year   *__No__*
c) Changed schools in mid-year   *__No__*
d) Began school year at a new school   *__No__*

Briefly describe how this child is doing in school. Note current marks and areas of strength or weakness in school work. *__Keeva has always done excellent work in school. She is an "A" student.__*

Has he/she had any remedial help or special education services in school or privately? If so please describe and give approximate dates. *__No__*

Please describe this child's attitude toward school. Note any special interests or dislikes he/she has in school. *__Keeva likes school and is almost never absent. She has many interests and talents.__*

How does this child get along with the teacher and other students in school? *__Until this year, Keeva has been very popular with her peers. Now she seems to withdraw from social interactions with her friends.__*

SOCIAL DEVELOPMENT/PEER RELATIONSHIPS

What special interests, hobbies, sports and games does the child enjoy both in and after school? *Dance, gymnastics*

When this child chooses playmates are they:

older   younger   *own age*   all ages

boys   girls   *both boys and girls*

In play activities is the child a leader, a follower or a loner? *Keeva was always a leader*

Does the child prefer the company of adults to other children?   Yes_____ No **X**

Does the child have at least one best friend   Yes **X**   No _____
What is the friend's age? *Same age*

EMOTIONAL DEVELOPMENT

Has your child ever been characterized by family members, teachers or others as being:

	Yes No		Yes No
Restless/ inattentive	*No*	Forgetful	*No*
Humorous/fun	*Yes*	Quick to anger	*Yes-recently*
Cheerful	*Yes*	Depressed/sad	*Yes- recently*
Daydreamer	*No*	Disruptive	*No*
Immature	*No*	Happy	*Yes- but not lately*
Aggressive	*No*	Nervous/tense	*Yes-recently*

Does this child have a great many fears or worries. If so, what are they?_____
Keeva worries about being fat and getting good grades.

Does the child have unusual or persistent nightmares? If so, what are they about? *Keeva has not had nightmares that we are aware of.*

SPECIAL CONCERNS

Briefly describe this child's behavior at home *Keeva has been difficult to live with for the last several months since we discovered her eating disorder. She refuses to eat and exercises constantly. She resists everything we say and seems sad and depressed most of the time. Sometimes she is so irritable that it is difficult to be in the same house with her.*

Please check below any past or present concerns; then give the age during which they occurred. (Example: Eating......from 4-6 years).

Area of Difficulty	Age From	To	Area of Difficulty	Age From	To
Speech			Destructiveness		
Eating	*12- 13 years*		Physical Health	*12-13 years*	
Sleeping			Fears	*12-13 years*	
Activity Level	*12-13 years*		Bladder Control		
Coordination			Bowel Function		
Aggressiveness			Temper Tantrums	*12- 13 years*	
Sexual Activity			Lying		
Response to Discipline			Stealing		
Relationship to Peers			Firesetting		
Ability to Learn			Thumb Sucking		
School Adjustment			Tics		
Play Behavior			Drugs		
Anxiety *12-13 years*			Truancy		
Degree of Responsibility			Other		

Please elaborate on any concerns that you have about any of the difficulties listed *Since Keeva has developed this eating disorder, she seems to have a great deal of fear about "being fat." When we try to get her to eat, she has temper tantrums and refuses. Although she was always exercising, she seems to have increased the level of exercise beyond normal limits while decreasing her intake of food.*

Describe special strengths that the child has shown in his or her overall adjustment to past difficulties. *Keeva has always been a fighter who hangs with something until she accomplishes it. She is bright and has a cheerful and polite manner that endears her to others. She has many friends and family members as supporters.*

FAMILY RELATIONSHIPS/HISTORY

Please list **all** family members currently living at home or closely connected with the family. Indicate their ages, relationship to this child (e.g. sister, step-brother, aunt, etc. and their school grade or occupation. Include parents who are currently living with the child.

Name	Age	Relationship	Grade or Occupation
Jane M.	35	Mother	Owns art gallery
John M.	38	Father	CEO Int'l Plastics
Mary M.	68	Paternal Grandmother	Retired Teacher

Have any of the following potential problems been present in your (the parents') original families, previous family if remarried and/ or your current family? If so state which family unit(s) experienced the problem {mother's (M), father's (F), previous family (P), and/or current family (C)}.

(C)	Career involvement, Father	_____	Multiple moves
(C)	Career involvement, Mother	_____	Financial pressures
_____	Physical health of family member(s)	_____	Marital problems
_____	Mental health of family member(s)	(M)	Separation or Divorce
_____	Death of special family member	(C)	Prolonged Absence
(C)	Differences in child-rearing	_____	Drinking

RELATIONSHIPS

How does this child get along with his/her brothers and/or sisters? *Keeva has no brothers or sisters*

Describe any special activities that you do with this child. *Keeva's father usually spends weekends doing special things with her. These outings have been less frequent in the past year because of his travel schedule.*

If you were to describe your child as a person and **not** as a son or daughter, what would you say about him or her? *Keeva is a sensitive young lady who wants very much to please her family and who has the misguided notion that she is too fat to be attractive. She seems to crave love and approval.*

SIGNATURE(S) OF PARENT(S) WHO COMPLETED THIS FORM

Father: *John M.*   Date *2-12-96*
Mother: *Jane M.*   Date *2-12-96*

The case conference is an important part of the team approach to assessment and treatment planning. This multidisciplinary approach enables the treatment team to develop goals and suggest strategies and activities that each team member can accomplish. Generally, the team is led by the case manager who can be a counselor, psychologist, social worker, physician, nurse, or other human services professional. The following case conference procedure and worksheet is intended to assist practitioners in assessing Keeva's current physical and mental health and developing a plan of intervention. A worksheet is also provided for those students who wish to learn more about making a DSM-IV diagnosis.

Case Conference Procedure

A.   Collect information

B.   Invite appropriate people

C.   Conduct meeting

   a. State reasons for the meeting

   b. Identify behaviors of concern

   c. Present factual data

   d. Solicit factual information from participants

   e. Encourage participants to react to what has been presented and collect additional data

   f. Seek interpretation of data from each participant's perspective

   g. Develop a plan of intervention

D.   Organize intervention strategies and activities

E.   Follow-up

Worksheet for Case Conference

A. **Data presented by each participant:**

B. **Reactions to data presented:**

C. **Interpretation of data:**

a. Child Strengths/Potential Strengths

1. **Positive aspects of child's behavior**

2. **Positive aspects of family behavior/background**

3. **Positive impact of significant others**

4. **Positive impact of school and community**

Worksheet for Case Conference

b. Negative Factors/Potential Negative Factors

    l. Potential consequences of child's negative behavior

    2. Family behavior/background liabilities

    3. Negative impacts of school and community

CONCLUSIONS:

D. Intervention Strategies/Activities

    1. Home

    2. School

    3. Community

E. Suggestions for Intervention Follow-up

DSM-IV DIAGNOSIS *

Keeva M.

AXIS I **Clinical Disorders**
Other Conditions That May Be a Focus of Clinical Attention

Code **DSM-IV Name**

_____ _____

_____ _____

AXIS II **Personality Disorders**
Mental Retardation

_____ _____

_____ _____

AXIS III **General Medical Conditions**

_____ _____

_____ _____

AXIS IV **Psychosocial and Environmental Problems**

Specify _____

_____

_____

AXIS V: Global Assessment of Functioning Scale **Score_____**

* From: American Psychiatric Association, *Diagnostic and Statistical Manual of Mental Disorders: Fourth Edition (DSM-IV),* Washington, D.C.: Author (refer to pages 25-35).

Treatment Plan: Keeva M.

This treatment plan should contain provisions for addressing all of Keeva's developmental needs. Use a team approach to this plan and assume your role (e.g., psychologist, counselor, social worker, nurse) as a member of the team. Specific treatment goals should be outlined for Keeva *and* her family.

Goals

_____

_____

_____

_____

Strategy/Activity

_____

_____

_____

_____

Participants

_____

_____

_____

_____

Media Suggestions

Books

Arent, R.P. (1992). *Trust Building with Children Who Hurt: A One-to-One Support Program for Children Ages 5 to 14.* West Nyack, NY: The Center for Applied Research in Education.

This helpful guide to building trust with child clients is a must read for counselors, teachers and other human services professionals. It offers a program designed for children (and teens) that builds on existing self-esteem and competence. It offers a "Struggles Chart" as a way to note ongoing problems, strengths, and improvements.

Herskowitz, J. (1990). *Is Your Child Depressed?* New York: Warner Books.

This is a handbook for parents. It can help you decide whether your child is depressed and in need of treatment. The emphasis is on psychotherapy as a primary form of treatment with medication as a last resort.

McKnew, D.H. & Crytryn, L. (1983). *Why Isn't Johnny Crying: Coping With Depression in Children.* New York: W. W. Norton.

Often depressed individuals have trouble expressing emotion. This book helps identify the symptoms of depression in children and find diagnosis and treatment for depressive disorders.

Reaves, J. & Austin, J.B. (1990). *How to Find Help for a Troubled Kid: A Parent's Guide to Programs and Services for Adolescents.* New York: Holt.

The first sourcebook for parents who know their child needs help but don't know how to find it. Includes information on Learning Centers, Therapy, Juvenile Justice System, Special Camps, Half-Way Houses, Hot Lines, Adventure and Survival Programs, and more. This reassuring and authoritative book helps families find the help that they need.

Wood, M.M. & Long, N.J. (1991). *Life Space Intervention.* Austin, TX: Pro-Ed.

This book teaches the unique skills of interviewing children and youth during interpersonal crises. It offers five types of therapeutic interventions that are beneficial to children in conflict. It is designed for human services professionals who work with children who have special needs.

Inventories/Tests

Battle, J. (1992). *Culture-Free Self-Esteem Inventories* (CRSEI). Austin, TX: Pro-Ed.

The CRSEI consists of self-report scales that are used to determine the level of self-esteem in children and adults. Children's self-esteem is measured by five scales which include: general, peers, school, parents, and defensiveness (lie scale). These inventories can be administered individual or in groups in a variety of settings and in many cultural and linguistic environments.

Brown, L. & Hammill, D.D. (1990). *Behavior Rating Profile* (BRP-2) (2nd ed.). Austin, TX: Pro-Ed.

Designed for ages 6 years 6 months through 18 years 6 months, the BRP -2 provides different evaluations of a student's behavior at home, at school, and in interpersonal relationships from the varied perspectives of parents, teachers, peers, and the identified children themselves. The responses allow practitioners to test different hypotheses when confronted with reports of problem behavior.

Gilliam, J. E. (1995). *Attention-Deficit/Hyperactivity Disorder Test: A Method for Identifying Individuals with ADHD* (ADHDT). Austin, TX: Pro-Ed.

This instrument identifies and evaluates ADHD in persons age 3 to 23. Normed in 1993 and 1994, it offers the most current norms available. Kit includes examiner's manual and 50 summary response forms.

Kovacs, M. (1992). *Children's Depression Inventory (CDI).* Austin, TX: Pro-Ed.

This self-report, symptom-oriented scale consists of 27 items that measure five factors related to depression. It is designed for school-age children and adolescents and can be administered individually or in groups. It can be used in schools, child guidance clinics, hospital and psychiatric settings, and other clinical and nonclinical settings.

Videos

Communicating with Preschoolers. (1995). Insight Media, 2162 Broadway, New
York, NY 10024.

Specific techniques to improve communication with young children are presented.
Child development experts discuss preschoolers' level of understanding and demonstrate
ways to talk with children and encourage them to express their feelings.

Valuing Diversity: Multicultural Communication.(1994). Insight Media, 2162
Broadway, New York, NY 10024.

Through dramatizations, this video demonstrates how to overcome cross-cultural
communication barriers. It teaches verbal and nonverbal communication skills. This
program also considers how cultural stereotyping can lead to inaccurate judgments. (19
minutes)

Chapter 5

Individual and Group Counseling with Children

This chapter focuses on implementing the treatment plan discussed in Chapter 4. Treatment goals, developed through the assessment process, are realized in the counseling of the individual child or in group counseling. Therefore, in this chapter, therapeutic process is examined and key factors presented. Integration of process and skills in individual and group counseling with children are explained, and examples of the application of the counseling process are provided.

Learning Objectives

Upon the completion of this chapter, you will be able to:

1. Describe the therapeutic process and identify key factors.

2. Outline special issues in counseling.

3. Define developmental group counseling and discuss its value.

4. Identify and explain the stages of the development of group process.

5. List group guidance activities and give examples of how they are incorporated into the counseling process.

Review Exercises

1. Identify the three areas that most child counselors, regardless of orientation, are concerned with in helping children.

2. List and describe five stages in the therapeutic process.

3. What are the key factors in the therapeutic process? Give an example of each.

4. How are problems analyzed by the child in the therapeutic process? What is the counselor's role?

5. Describe the process of internalization as a catalyst for change.

6. What are the advantages for counselors and for children in the group counseling setting?

7. Define developmental group counseling and identify related characteristics.

8. What is the value of group counseling?

9. List and describe the stages of group process development.

10. How are children selected for group counseling, and how are their needs assessed?

11. How is the size of the group determined?

12. When does a group appropriately end?

13. What is accomplished through large-group activities?

14. What types of activities are compatible in large-group settings?

Awareness Exercises

1. Read "A Bit of Background" in the beginning of the chapter. According to Hansen, Rossberg, and Cramer's 1994 book, almost all counseling approaches have certain commonalities. Do one or more of these statements hold any special significance or attraction to you? Why?

2. Read through the section on self-protective behaviors. Is there a behavior mentioned that you think you would have the most problems with in the counseling process? Why? Can you identify any of the resistance behaviors as those that you might have displayed in childhood?

3. Special issues related to the counseling process are outlined in this chapter. Having read this chapter, what might your response be to a child who says; "Do I have to be bad to come to see you? What would you actually say and/or do?

4. Are you concerned about becoming "too" attached to the child-client? Why or why not?

5. If you have an evolving preference, is it for individual or group counseling? Why?

6. Of the activities listed in this chapter, such as puppetry, games, unfinished stories, art activities, music, storytelling, books, writing, and sociodrama, for which do you feel particularly drawn or have talent?

Practical Applications
" School Stinks!": The Case of Monty P.

Ten-year-old Montgomery (Monty) is in the third grade. He lives in an intact family with his two sisters, Melodi, age 7 and Molly, age 12. During her pregnancy with Monty, Mrs. P. encountered some medical problems which necessitated a Caesarian delivery. Monty's early development was marked by irregular developmental milestones; he did not crawl but started walking at 15 months and he did not speak until age 2 1/2 when he suddenly began using words in sentences. Monty's preschool vocabulary was well developed because his mother read to him and his sisters on a daily basis. However, when his mother tried to get Monty to read at about age 6, he avoided it and she did not pressure him. Monty's father had some difficulty reading as a child and told his son that it was "OK" if he did not want to read.

In addition to problems with reading, Monty has had difficulties with coordination. He fell off his new bike so frequently that he gave up riding it. Despite urging from his father, Monty continually refuses to play catch or to do any physical activities. His mother has stopped asking him to help her set the table because he has broken so many plates and glasses. His sisters, who are talented in athletics, are embarrassed by Monty's clumsiness.

Initially, Monty loved kindergarten. He especially loved playing with clay and was extremely creative. However, Monty began to dislike kindergarten when the teacher made each child responsible for learning a letter of the alphabet and recognizing it in a word. At the end of each week, each child got a special star sticker for the completion of the task. Monty could not recognize a letter when it was put on the board, much less recognize a word. Many of the children made fun of him and called him "stupid" and "dumb." At the end of the year, Monty had the least number of stickers. Rather than be promoted to first grade, he was placed in a pre-first grade class.

As Monty has progressed in school, his progress reports have been increasingly filled with U's (unsatisfactory marks). He continues to mix up his b's and d's and cannot read. He rarely turns in his homework and when he does, it's messy. He is unable to tell time and his parents have provided him with a digital watch. Because he is unable to succeed in school, Monty has become a discipline problem and has been sent to the principal's office numerous times for disrupting class.

Recently, the third-grade teacher assigned parts for a play that the class was performing for Parents' Night. Monty was chosen as one of the main characters because the teacher thought that this activity would "tame" his disruptive behavior. When Monty learned of his role in the play, he begged and pleaded with his teacher and his parents to let him have a smaller nonreading part. Ignoring his pleas, the adults told him: "You'll do fine." On the night of the play, Monty stood in the front of the room, tried to improvise and failed miserably. Frustrated and embarrassed, Monty vowed never to return to school.

Since then, Mrs. P. has had to "do battle" with Monty every morning to get him to go to school. He usually complains that he is sick. If that doesn't work, he cries and tells his mother that "school stinks" and he won't go. Monty's sisters, although usually kind, complain that their mother is babying him by letting him stay home.

Counseling Skills: Definitions and Exercises

All counseling approaches acknowledge the need for a relationship in which the client will feel accepted, respected and understood. It is generally believed that the therapeutic conditions of congruence, unconditional positive regard and empathy, first described by Carl Rogers, are essential to the counseling relationship. Robert Carkhuff developed and refined a model of helping that built on the work of Carl Rogers. The Carkhuff model included the helping skills of attending, responding, personalizing, and initiating. Recent models, such as those developed by Gerard Egan, include advanced levels of empathy, concreteness, immediacy, and confrontation. For a more in-depth presentation of individual and group counseling skills, consult *The Skilled Helper* by Gerard Egan and Theory and *Practice of Group Counseling* by Gerald Corey. Complete references for these books can be found under Media Suggestions.

Active Listening

Coming in contact with an adult that truly *listens* is a treasured experience for a child. Part of listening is caring about children and wanting to help them. This attitude of warmth and acceptance is conveyed to the child through verbal and nonverbal attending, as well as through listening. The counselor's posture, facial expressions, gestures, and eye contact let children know that he or she is attending. Listening skills include restating, focusing on the feelings behind the child's words, asking questions, and allowing for brief silences. Both listening and attending skills are used to understand the meaning of the child's verbal and nonverbal communication.

Responding to Feelings and Communicating Empathy

Empathy involves capturing the essence of the child's feelings and formulating a response that communicates an understanding of the experiences and behaviors that accompany these feelings. By viewing a particular thought, feeling, or behavior from the child's perspective, the counselor is able to respond to the child on a deeper level, to encourage self-exploration, and to help the child toward greater self-understanding. Acceptance, respect, and empathic understanding engender feelings of trust in the relationship that lay the groundwork for change.

Example of Responding to Feeling and Communicating Empathy

Monty: I hate this place. . .(*slams his fist down and crosses his arms defiantly.*) It stinks!

CO: You sound angry and fed up with the way you are being treated at school.

Your Response:

_____

_____

Restating

This skill is an extension of active listening and focuses on the message behind the child's words. By paraphrasing the child's message, the counselor provides both support and clarification. Restating also gives the child a chance to react to the counselor's understanding of his or her message. Frequently children will say, "No! That isn't what I meant."

Example of Restating

    Monty: The teacher says 'try' but I do try and I can't. . .

    CO: You try very hard but you still can't do some of the work that is required.

    Your Response:

_____

_____

Open-Ended Questions

Open-ended questions can be used to encourage children to talk about their concerns; elaborate on their thoughts, feelings, and experiences or focus on a plan of action. A good rule is to avoid "why" questions, which put children on the defensive, as well as "closed questions, " which often result in one-word answers. For example, the counselor who asks, "Do you like school?" risks getting "Nope" as an answer. And the counselor who wants to know "_Why_ don't you like school?" frequently gets "I dunno" as a response.

Example of Open-Ended Question

    Monty: I told her I didn't want to be in any dumb play but she made me. I hate my teacher!

    CO: Would you like to tell me more about what happened?

    Your Response:

_____

_____

Clarifying

Clarifying involves using verbal and nonverbal listening skills to help the child bring his or her own thoughts and feelings into sharper focus. By asking clarifying questions or making statements, the counselor can help the child achieve a deeper level of self-understanding. An example of a clarifying question is, "Have you felt that way for a long time?"

Example of a Clarifying Response

Monty: If my parents keep making me come here, I'm gonna run away.

CO: You are upset with your parents for making you come to school when you are so unhappy here.

Your Response:

_____

_____

Summarizing

Summarizing the most significant aspects of the session into a few words enables the child to hear and think about the feelings and experiences that he or she has just expressed. In this way, the child is able to focus on particular issues and draw conclusions about his or her own strengths and weaknesses. When used properly, summarizing is a useful way to pull together the various themes of the session, to focus on relevant feelings and experiences, to encourage the child to explore important issues more fully and to bring closure to the session.

Challenging

Challenging is a form of confrontation that involves listening carefully enough so that you hear inconsistences in what a child says and does. Counselors should **gently** challenge the discrepancies between the child's words and actions. This skill is most effective when it is used in the later stages of the counseling process and after rapport and trust have been well established. It is important not to confront too early, especially if the child is emotionally vulnerable. In addition, some children, who avoid expressing their feelings, need to know that they are free to tell the counselor how they feel.

Example of a Challenging Response

Monty: I told my teacher that I didn't want to be in any dumb play but she made me. I hate her!

CO: I would be angry if a teacher forced me to do something that I couldn't do.

Monty: I was boiling mad. . . she knows I hate to read and she made me take a reading part.. What's the big deal about reading anyway? My dad can't read and he does OK.

CO: It sounds like you are angry with your teacher but you are also worried about being able to read.

Your Response:

_____

_____

Interpreting

Through interpretation, the counselor attempts to put what the child discloses into a more understandable framework so that the child can see the reasons for his or her feelings or behavior. These open-ended verbal sharings can be in the form of *tentative hypotheses,* i.e., "Could it be. . . " and should be geared to the child's needs and capacity for abstract thought (see Chapter 2). Interpretive responses require a level of cognitive reasoning and insight that is usually not found in younger children. Therefore, clarifying responses, "as-if" scenarios, and identifying and exploring themes in the child's expressions may be more appropriate ways of helping children to identify, label, and understand their feelings.

"As-if" scenarios, as described by Kevin O'Connor in *The Play Therapy Primer*, can be used to help children to own feelings that may be intensely threatening. To help children identify and talk about feelings that they may be hesitate to own, the counselor may word the response "as if" the feeling belonged to a group of children rather than the child client (e.g., " Some kids get very upset when their parents drink.") A variation of this technique is for the counselor to own the feeling (e.g., "I would be very angry if my Dad promised to take me someplace and then didn't show up").

Example of an "As-If" Scenario

Monty: You know my parents forced me to be in the play. If they
            keep doing this, I'm outta here!

CO: Some kids might feel embarrassed if their parents forced them
      to take a reading part in a play, especially if reading was hard
      for them.

Your Response:

_____

_____

Helping children understand the hidden meaning behind their messages can sometimes be accomplished by identifying and exploring themes or patterns in their communication. These themes can include the child's mood and affect, needs, desires, or behaviors and can be expressed directly or indirectly through words or symbols. Interpretation of the symbolism in the child's communication requires an in-depth knowledge of the child and his or her world. Recognizing these themes and sharing them with the child is a way of helping the child develop insight.

Example of an Interpretive Response

Monty: I was boiling mad. . .she knows I hate to read and she made
me take a reading part.

CO: Could it be that you are angry at your teacher because you
were embarrassed to read in front of an audience?

Your Response:

_____

_____

Encouraging

Encouragement is an important aspect of all phases in the therapeutic process but it is especially valuable as children begin to experience the power of their own inner resources. In order to hold on to the gains made in therapy, the child needs encouragement and support. Encouragement can instill feelings of worth, power, and control in children.

Example of an Encouraging Response

Monty: I'm just not good in school. . . I can't. . .

CO: You have been tellling me about your trouble with reading
but we haven't talked about your great grades in math.

Your Response:

_____

_____

Group Guidance Activities

All children should be free to choose whether or not they want to participate in group activities, and they should **never** be forced to play out a personal problem in front of the class. **A child should not be chosen to play a role that is too close to what he or she is experiencing in real life, even if the child volunteers for the part.** In the following scenarios, Monty could be selected (if he volunteers) to role play the part of the parent or another child who is **not** experiencing any learning problems. In this way, he will not risk feeling worse instead of better, and he will have an opportunity to rebuild his tattered self-esteem.

Suggested Activities:

1. Encourage the children to plan a puppet play that revolves around helping a brother or sister who has difficulty reading.

2. Using the cardboard family puppets, ask the children to role play what *they* would do if they were parents and their "children" refused to go to school. Encourage the youngsters to talk to their "pretend children" about school.

3. Ask children to draw themselves. Then ask them to draw themselves doing something at school. Use these drawings as an opening to discuss what the children like and dislike about daily life at school.

4. Read one of the books listed in Chapter 8 that deals with learning disabilities. Facilitate a discussion on some of the problems that children have that make them feel different and unhappy at school.

Media Suggestions

Books

Corey, G. (1995). *Theory and Practice of Group Counseling* (4th ed.). Pacific
Grove, CA: Brooks/Cole.

In a thoroughly readable text, Corey describes the stages in the group process
and the skills that the group leader uses to facilitate change. Excellent examples help the
reader understand how the group process works.

Egan, G. (1994). *The Skilled Helper: A Problem-Management Approach to
Helping* (5th ed.). Pacific Grove, CA: Brooks/Cole.

An overview of the counseling model is presented, along with all of the basic
communication skills for helping. Excellent examples guide the reader in understanding
each step of the process.

Hansen, J.C., Rossberg, R.H. & Cramer, S.H. (1994). *Counseling: Theory
and Process* (5th. ed.). Boston, MA: Allyn & Bacon.

Excellent explanations are offered for all of the major counseling approaches.
Chapters 12 and 13 are especially helpful for readers who want to know more about
counseling as a relationship.

Thompson, C.L. & Rudolph, L.B. (1996). *Counseling Children* (4th ed.).
Pacific Grove, CA: Brooks/Cole.
This comprehensive text offers a view of child counseling from all of the major
theoretical perspectives. Excerpts from counseling transcripts illustrate how each is
applied in practice. Relevant research in the field of child counseling is also included.

Videos

Basic Interviewing Skills for Psychologists. (1991). Insight Media, 2162 Broadway, New York, NY. 10024.

This film presents a series of vignettes that focus on specific communication techniques for interviewing clients. Based on the principles of social-learning theory, five basic skills-- listening, reflecting, questioning, expressing and interpreting-- are taught in various segments. The firm concludes with a session in which all counseling skills are integrated. (51 minutes)

Microcounseling Skills. (1992). Insight Media, 2162 Broadway, New York, NY. 10024.

Using sample counseling sessions, this video presents the skills of observing, questioning, showing empathy, focusing, interpreting, and confronting. Based on Ivey's philosophy of microcounseling, the program demonstrates both effective and ineffective ways to handle different counseling situations. (2 volumes, 150 min. total)

Rational-Emotive Therapy with Children and Adolescents. (1991) Insight Media, 2162 Broadway, New York, NY. 10024.

Two actual sessions are presented using rational-emotive therapy with children and adolescents. In the first session, Dr. Michael Bernard works with a 10-year-old girl who is struggling with low self-acceptance. The second session is with a 15-year-old boy who is having difficulties at school as a result of anger and depression. (105 min.)

Treating Time Effectively: First Session in Brief Therapy. (1993). Insight Media, 2162 Broadway, New York, NY. 10024.

This video focuses on time-effective therapy and examines the issues that requiretherapeutic attention. In addition to the therapeutic relationship, it considers problem selection and scheduling.

Chapter 6
Play Therapy

A counseling strategy, play therapy, is the focus of this chapter. The developmental stages of play are discussed and the foundation is laid for introducing play as therapy. Theoretical perspectives related to play as therapy are also presented. The chapter describes play therapy techniques and the play process. The underlying theme in the discussion of play therapy is that play facilitates the child's growth and development and therefore is a significant resource for use as a counseling strategy.

Learning Objectives

Upon completion of this chapter, you will be able to:

1. Describe the developmental stages of child's play.

2. Characterize the theoretical perspectives from which play therapy evolved.

3. Explain the value of play therapy.

4. Select appropriate toys and materials for use in play therapy that will facilitate the child's communication and the realizing of therapeutic objectives.

5. Describe how techniques and materials can be utilized by directive and nondirective counselors, regardless of their counseling orientation.

6. Identify the stages of the therapeutic play process.

Review Exercises

1. Outline the historical development of play.

2. List and describe the developmental stages in child's play.

3. Compare and contrast the following theorists with respect to their view on play therapy:

   Melanie Klein, Anna Freud, David Levy, Gove Hambridge, Otto Rank, Allan Moustakas, Virginia Axline, Bernard and Louise Guerney.

4. Describe the current trends related to play therapy theory and application.

5. What is the value of play therapy?

6. Comment on the value of play therapy for children who are withdrawn, nonverbal, wounded, and/or unable to express their feelings in words.

7. List toys that might be used to achieve specific therapeutic goals:

   a) Facilitate Expression
   b) Encourage Creativity
   c) Release Emotion
   d) Express Aggression

8. Describe the use of the following play therapy techniques and related materials in the counseling process:

   Doll Play; Puppet Play; Sand Play; Game Playing.

9. What are the five stages of the play therapy process?

10. Identify the special issues that present challenges to the counselor in play therapy.

11. How would the therapist respond to the child's question; "Why am I here?"

12. How would the counselor respond to the child's interest in wanting to know things about the counselor's personal life?

13. How would the counselor set limits regarding time spent in play, taking toys from the playroom, or wanting food or drink?

14. In the case of traumatic grief involving Clinton, age 6 and Clay, age 4, how did the counselor arrive at the treatment goals, and why were the specific treatment strategies/ play activities selected?

Awareness Exercises

1. React to the statement in the "Bit of Background," last paragraph: " Regardless of economic background, today's children are not often encouraged to be creative and imaginative in play." Do you agree or disagree? State your reasons.

2. What do you remember about play in your childhood? Did you have some favorite toys? Can you remember any particular incidents with special toys. . . lost, broken, or other? What do you remember feeling?

3. Now that you are a grown-up, the type of play you engage in has changed, and the "toys" have changed. Do you take time to play now? How do you identify play as an adult? What value do you ascribe to play?

4. Choose a toy from the play therapy room, if accessible, or borrow a toy from a friend or relative. Why do you think you chose this particular toy? Journal how it feels to play with it. Can you identify with any of the stages of play therapy in your own play, such as releasing feelings, etc. ?

5. Can you imagine yourself as a counselor using this strategy (play therapy) and being comfortable with it?

Practical Applications

"God Made My Bones Bad" The Case of Christian B.

Christian is a 7-year-old boy of average intelligence who is in the second grade. He lives in an intact, devoutly religious family. His mother, Ann, is a teacher at the local high school and his father, Graden, is a psychiatrist. Christian has a twin sister Noelle, an older brother Bennett, age 13 , and a younger brother Grady, who is three. Christian looks up to Bennett, and the two boys share a room in a large home in a quiet suburban community. Family members are described as close-knit and they enjoy doing things together. The children especially enjoy their pets, which include two dogs and a family of gold fish.

While playing baseball with his older brother, Christian suddenly fell over, seemingly crippled with pain. He was taken to the emergency room for X-rays and other medical tests. The results of this preliminary work revealed that Christian's bones were normal; however, his joints were abnormally swollen. A medical and developmental history, given by his mother, indicated that Christian had experienced no previous physical problems and none were present in the family's history. However, Christian's mother reported that he had been having high fevers in the last few months and that he had recently developed a transient pink rash. Christian was admitted to the hospital for extensive testing, which included an examination of his bone marrow. On the basis of the test results and the symptoms described by Christian's mother, a diagnosis of juvenile rheumatoid arthritis was made.

Juvenile rheumatoid arthritis is a serious, chronic disease with an onset before age 16. It may appear between the ages of 1 and 3 for young children or between the ages of 7 and 12 for school-age children. This relatively rare disease can be difficult to assess, and there are no laboratory tests that definitively establish the diagnosis. Children with arthritis have swollen and painful joints that are warm to the touch. The affected joints are severely limited in their range of motion. This disease is treated by controlling the painful symptoms with medication as well as by preventing permanent deformity through physical therapy. In many cases, the disease becomes quiescent as the children reach adulthood, and they can eventually lead normal lives.

After the diagnosis of juvenile rheumatoid arthritis was confirmed, the pediatrician and orthopedic specialist sat down with Christian and his parents and tried to explain his condition in terms that he could understand. He was told that he would have to stay in the hospital for about a month. After this session, Christian withdrew; staying in his room and refusing to eat or talk with anyone. The following day, Christian refused to talk to his brother when he came to visit, despite the fact that the two had always been best friends. Later, Christian told the play therapist that "God made my bones bad because I was playing with Bennett instead of doing my chores." The therapist tried to ease his anxiety, but Christian was convinced that he had been "bad" and that God was angry with him for disobeying his mother.

Christian is convinced that his illness is somehow his fault and that God has cursed him with a disease because he behaved badly. He also has considerable anxiety about being in the hospital for a month, about his treatment, and about being separated from his family. Last, Christian has expressed the fear that he might die. These are all normal behaviors for hospitalized children and can be dealt with successfully in therapy. In addition, Christian's doctors believe that his prognosis is hopeful.

1. Identify the strengths of Christian and his family that will help him cope with his illness and hospitalization?

_____

_____

_____

2. Which play therapy techniques (e.g., storytelling, writing, game playing, puppetry, and/or doll play) would you use to help Christian understand and deal with his feelings of guilt and anxiety? Describe in detail how you think the technique you selected could help.

_____

_____

_____

3. As the practitioner, would you include Bennett in any of the play therapy sessions? Would you include the entire family? Choose a particular play therapy technique and describe how it would lend itself to family therapy.

_____

_____

_____

Media Suggestions

Books

Axline, V.M. (1947). *Play Therapy.* New York: Ballantine Books.

This classic work provides students with specific illustrations of how to conduct nondirective play therapy. Using dialogue from real cases, Axline demonstrates that play can be an integral part of the therapeutic process. This book, treasured by therapists, is invaluable to parents, teachers and anyone who comes into contact with children.

Crowley, R.J. & Mills, J.C. (1989). *Cartoon Magic: How to Help Children Discover Their Rainbow Within.* New York: Magination Press.

Here is a therapeutic technique for parents to use with young children to help them resolve concerns such as nightmares, hospital visits, or the loss of a friend or a pet. All you will need is paper, pencils, a problem to be solved, and an ability to enter the child's "land of pretend."

Gil, E. (1994). *Play in Family Therapy.* New York: Guilford Press.

This well-written and riveting book provides case illustrations using family puppet interviews, family art therapy, and storytelling techniques. The final chapter provides additional creative play techniques that Dr. Gil has found helpful in therapy with children and their families.

Schaefer, C.E. & Reid, S.E. (Eds). (1986). *Game Play:Therapeutic Use of Childhood Games.* New York: Wiley.

Game Play highlights the importance of using games to assess and treat children with various childhood problems. It features games that promote communication, problem solving skills, enhance self-esteem, and foster socialization.

Books

Schaefer, C.E. & Cangelosi, D.M. (Eds.). (1993). *Play Therapy Techniques.* Northvale, NJ:
> Jason Aronson

This collection of play therapy techniques includes art, puppet, sand, dramatic, water, doll, costume, and game play. It includes both classic and recent approaches and contains explicit "how to" procedures to guide both novice and experienced play therapists.

Webb, N. B. (Ed.). (1991). *Play Therapy with Children in Crisis: A Casebook for Practitioners.* New York: The Guilford Press.

This invaluable casebook demonstrates how a variety of play techniques can be used to help children resolve crises related to the death of a parent, marital separation and divorce, violence, medical emergencies, war and natural disasters. In-depth examples are provided that permit the reader to follow the therapeutic process from beginning to end.

Videos

Techniques of Play Therapy: *A Clinical Demonstration.* (1994). Insight Media, 2162 Broadway, New York, NY. 10024.

Play therapy is illustrated as a natural method for engaging, assessing and communicating therapeutically with children. A wide range of treatment strategies are presented that are appropriate for children ages 4 to 12. This video illustrates the use of clay, drawing, puppets, blocks, and board games as a part of play therapy.

Chapter 7
Art Therapy

This chapter focuses on the value of art as a therapeutic process. Background information is presented which traces children's art through developmental stages. The interpretation of art in child therapy is also discussed including techniques and symbolic content. Actual art activities are described and recommended for application as they particularly relate to individual, group and family therapy.

Learning Objectives

Upon completion of this chapter, you will be able to:

1. Explain the use and value of art therapy in various therapeutic contexts.

2. Present an overview of the developmental perspective (ages and stages) of children's art.

3. Discuss how the child's needs related to therapy can be assessed through art activities, and how diagnostic information can be solicited.

4. Appropriately apply the strategies presented for interpreting the child's art.

5. Suggest art activities for use in the individual, group, and family therapeutic process.

Review Exercises

1. How would you define art therapy?

2. List the types of settings in which art therapy can be used. What is the purpose of its use in each of these settings?

3. Contrast Naumberg's and Kramer's theories related to art therapy.

4. Comment on Kwiatkowska's contributions to family art therapy.

5. Characterize these developmental stages of children's art: a) scribbling b) picture c) human figure, d) realistic representation, and e) naturalistic.

6. What is the value of art as a therapeutic process?

7. What aspects of the child-counselor relationship are essential to the successful use of art in child therapy?

8. How are children's therapeutic needs assessed through their art?

9. List and describe the formal assessment tools that may be used in conjunction with free art.

10. Identify the techniques used to interpret the child's art.

11. Describe the "interpreting process."

12. According to Edith Kramer, five art activities are important to the art therapy process. List and explain each.

13. What factors are used to interpret *form* in children's art work?

14. What factors are used to interpret *content* in children's art work?

15. What factors are considered *symbolic content* of children's art work?

16. Why are children's drawings of family particularly significant? What factors are considered in interpreting these drawings?

17. How is the impression reached in "The Case of Ivan" that the monster he drew represents his fears and his wariness of a menacing and threatening environment?

18. List and explain five important values of art as a family group technique.

Awareness Exercises

1. Do you like to draw? When do you draw? What is the content? What are some of your feelings during and after drawing?

2. Do you have a favorite art form or particular artists you appreciate? What is the appeal for you?

3. Make the play dough and finger paint recipes (perhaps with a group of students). Since it has probably been a long time since you have used these medias, simply have fun. Feel the dough and paint and describe both the tactile and emotional feelings in your journal.

4. Draw your family and a self-portrait. Share your drawings with a classmate and talk about the colors that you used and the placement and the significance of the features that are included in your pictures. Use the guidelines presented in this chapter to help you interpret the representations.

Practical Applications

"I'll Be Dead Before You Know It": The Case of Kendra Q.

Kendra is 9 years old and she has AIDS. She is the second born in a family of four children. Her older brother, Rashad, is 10 and is not infected with HIV. A younger brother died of AIDS complications at the age of 14 months when Kendra was seven. Her younger sister is 4 years old and is HIV-positive. Kendra's mother married directly out of high school at age 19 and had her first son a year later. The relationship between Kendra's mother and father was beset by problems and both had extramarital affairs. Kendra's father was a known drug user who left the family shortly after learning that his youngest child had AIDS. He refused to be tested. He kept in contact with the children-- seeing them, writing, and calling about three times a month-- but there has been no word from him in the past four months or so.

Kendra was 3 years old when she was first diagnosed as HIV-positive. As an infant, Kendra experienced swelling of the lymph glands in the neck, under the arms, and in the diaper area. She had a swollen belly and a series of rashes on her body. She experienced a delay in achieving the developmental milestones of sitting, crawling, and walking. During the first year of life, Kendra was hospitalized six times for lung infections and complications stemming from an ear infection.

Kendra was told of her diagnosis shortly after her brother's death, and she seemed, at least on the surface, to handle it well. She had a lot of questions that her mother tried to answer. She spent a lot of time talking to her grandparents about where heaven was and what they thought death was like.

Lately Kendra has been acting out in class, throwing fits, and crying with no provocation. Academically, she has always performed above grade-level but her grades have dropped considerably during the past four months. She has difficulty concentrating in class and chooses to spend much of her time alone in the corner of the playground. During gym class, she refuses to participate in the activities, saying that she is "going to kill somebody and then nobody will like me."

Kendra was always described by her teachers as an "outgoing child with a creative personality" but they have noted that instead of doing the work assigned in class, she doodles tombstones and coffins in the corners of her papers. During sharing time, Kendra tends to direct the classroom topics to death and dying. She is very persistent in wanting the class to share with her their ideas about death and will cry or verbally attack other students if they try to change the topic.

Socially, Kendra has always been accepted among her classmates as a leader, but her teachers have noticed that lately Kendra refuses to participate in any of the children's games. If a friend asks Kendra to play, she looks as if she is afraid and starts to cry. Teachers have overheard her say, "My blood is poison, and if you don't let me have your sandwich, I'm going to bleed on you." After such a comment, Kendra will laugh and say she was either joking or not to worry because " I'll be dead before you know it."

At home, Kendra is quiet, occasionally talking to her oldest brother but rarely talking to her mother or sister. When her youngest brother was alive, Kendra spent a lot of time "nursing" him; and now that he has died, she complains that there is "nothing to do." Although she avoids direct contact with her younger sister, Kendra is always watching and making sure that she is all right. For example, Kendra has been known to sit outside her sister's door all night and to wake her brother if she hears her sister cough.

Kendra's mother says that Kendra will not talk to her, make eye contact or answer her questions. Mrs. Q. states that she doesn't remember the last time she had a conversation with Kendra and that she is generally forced to relay messages through her son. For example, Kendra usually ignores her mother if asked to set the table; however, if the request is made through Rashad, Kendra is usually cooperative. For the most part, Mrs. Q. allows Kendra to do anything she wants to and rarely interferes even when Kendra throws a tantrum. Instead, she gives in to almost everything.

Practical Application

During the counseling session, Kendra uses the black finger paint and smears it all over the page. She then places a spoonful of red finger paint on the edge of her paper. Using the red paint, she draws three crosses and three coffins. As she works, she comments: "My blood is poison . . .and I'll be dead before you know it."

1. List some emotions that come to mind as you think about Kendra's finger painting.

_____

_____

_____

2. How would you describe Kendra's mood and affect as reflected in her painting ?

_____

_____

_____

3. As Kendra's counselor, how would you respond to her statement "My blood is poison...and I'll be dead before you know it."

_____

_____

_____

4. Kendra tells the counselor that she doesn't go to Sunday school anymore because "God already hates me so why should I go?" As Kendra's counselor, how would you respond?

_____

_____

_____

5. Describe which of the grief stages of denial, anger, bargaining, depression and acceptance, identified by Kubler-Ross, are evident in Kendra's drawing and accompanying verbalizations?

_____

_____

_____

6. List some of your own feelings about what Kendra has painted. Can you identify with any of the thoughts, feelings, and behaviors expressed in Kendra's painting and in her verbalizations?

_____

_____

_____

7. In a final session, Kendra draws a picture of herself up in the clouds next to a small figure that she identifies as her brother: "I'd like to learn everything that I can in school so that when I die I can teach my baby brother how to read and write in the clouds. . . so we could let our mother know that we are okay and happy." How would you respond?

_____

_____

_____

Media Suggestions

Books

Handler, L. (1996) The Clinical Use of Drawings: Draw-A-Person, House-Tree-Person and Kinetic Family Drawings. In C.S. Newmark, *Major Psychological Assessment Instruments.* (2nd. ed., pp. 206-288). Boston, MA: Allyn & Bacon.

Chapter 6 of the text provides an excellent overview of the Draw-A-Person, House-Tree-Person, and Kinetic Family Drawing tests. The advantages, instructions, and interpretations for each are carefully explained. Numerous drawings help the reader understand various aspects of these projective techniques as assessment instruments.

Linesch, D. (1993). *Art Therapy with Families in Crisis: Overcoming Resistance Through Nonverbal Expression.* New York: Brunner/Mazel

This book addresses the connections between the creative process and the experience of family therapy. The book begins with a brief explanation of family systems and how the art experience becomes part of the therapeutic process. Specific chapters are included that detail family art therapy with single-parent families, alcoholic families, and political refugees.

Oster, G.D. & Gould, P. (1987). *Using Drawing in Assessment and Therapy: A Guide for Mental Health Professionals.* New York: Brunner/Mazel.

This handy manual is helpful for practitioners who want to understand more about using art in both assessment and therapy. In addition to giving the commonly accepted interpretations for human figure drawings, the authors offer some suggestions for interpreting other projective tests. An especially helpful chapter uses drawings as a group technique to help participants identify problems and goals, increase interaction, and build cohesiveness.

Chapter 8
Bibliotherapy

In this chapter, another counseling strategy is explored: bibliotherapy. The value of this strategy in child therapy and its relationship to the healing process are explained. Methods of assessing conflict and selecting appropriate books are examined. Child abuse, divorce, and exploring feelings are given as examples of counseling situations in which bibliotherapy can be applied. Books are helpful in exploring developmental concerns, understanding parents and families, and dealing with disabilities. Bibliotherapy is another technique that can be added to the therapist's repertoire in the counseling of children and their families.

Learning Objectives

Upon completion of this chapter, you will be able to:

1. Define bibliotherapy and discuss its value in child therapy.

2. List factors to consider in selecting books for children in therapy.

3. Apply techniques for using bibliotherapy in individual and small- and large-group sessions related to specific issues such as child abuse and divorce.

Review Exercises

1. How is bibliotherapy defined in the text?

2. What are the three basic differences between clinical and educational uses of bibliotherapy as described by Berry?

3. Explain the value of bibliotherapy in the counseling of children and their families.

4. Characterize the steps in the healing process that occurs in bibliotherapy.

5. What are the factors to be considered in selecting books for bibliotherapy?

6. Give five examples of the types of books used in counseling.

7. As children read or listen to a story, they experience identification, catharsis, and insight. Discuss the value of these three factors in counseling.

8. List five follow-up strategies that can be used in conjunction with bibliotherapy.

Awareness Exercises

1. Do you enjoy reading aloud? Do you enjoy reading to yourself? What types of books interest you?

2. What motivates you to read a certain book? List some books that have special significance for you and explain why.

3. Choose one of the books recommended for use in counseling and listed in this chapter under a specific category such as Growing Up, Common Developmental Problems, Understanding Parents and Families, Childhood Crises, and/or Dealing with Disabilities.

a) Choose one that has a particular interest for you: What is motivating your choice?

b) Read the book. Look at the illustrations. In your journal, write a short summary. Based on your own opinion, include an analysis regarding:

1. What feelings you have after reading this book.

2. Is your selection suitable for use in counseling with children? Which type of counseling issues does the book address? What ages do you think would be appropriate for the reading of this book?

3. What are the potential "uses" or "lessons" pertaining to identification, catharsis, or insight that a child reading this book might obtain?

4. Do you think this book is most suitable for use with children individually or in small or large groups?

5. Are there some books you might add to the list in this chapter that you think might be of use in counseling?

6. Can you remember any books that had particular significance to you in childhood? Titles? Reason why?

7. You might want to begin your own bibliotherapy library. Make a list of the books you would like to acquire that are of special interest to you.

Practical Applications

"I Was Scared!" The Case of Stewart S.

Stewart is the only child of Mr. and Mrs. S., who adopted him when they were both in their mid 40s. Mr. S. is an engineer at a local company and his wife works two days a week in the office. Stewart, who is intellectually gifted, has always been well-behaved. His parents enjoy his company and are proud of his academic and artistic accomplishments. Stewart has taken violin lessons since he was 5 and has played in numerous recitals. Stewart is praised often by his teachers for his fine manners and good behavior.

Lately, Stewart has been asking his mother to drive him to school. On the days that Mrs. S. works, Stewart feigns a fever so that he won't have to ride the bus. Because Stewart has always liked school, Mr. and Mrs. S. are puzzled and concerned about this sudden change in behavior. One day when she had to work, Mrs. S. insisted that Stewart ride the bus. He obeyed but when he got off the bus he was crying. He told his mother that a kid named Butch had grabbed his book bag and held it so he couldn't reach it. Butch then took some things out of the bag and threw the rest on the floor of the bus. When asked if he told anyone, Stewart replied, "No! I was too scared!" Later, Stewart summed up his predicament by saying, " I just know I'm going to get beat up!"

1. Identify the behaviors that concern you in this case. What developmental problem do these behaviors suggest (refer to Chapter 2)?

_____

_____

_____

" I'll Beat You Up!": The Case of "Butch" B.

Rhett B. is the youngest child in a family of seven children. He is named after his father but goes by his nickname, "Butch."   This name seems to fit this feisty youngster who has had to stand up for himself with his older brothers, ages 11, 12, and 13. The brothers often engage in fistfights, and Butch usually gets the worst of it because his brothers are bigger and stronger. His three older sisters, all teenagers, admit that they spoil him and acquiesce to his demands.

When Butch entered school, he learned that he could win fights.   All of the practice that he had fist-fighting with his brothers came in handy when he fought with kids his own size. Soon Butch learned that all he had to do was *threaten* some kids, especially those who were smaller and weaker, and he could get what he wanted. He frequently would see a boy or girl in the neighborhood who had something he wanted, such as a toy or an ice cream cone, and he would say,   "Give me that or I'll beat you up!"

When the school notified Butch's parents that he was getting into fights and threatening other children, Mr. B   punished him with a spanking. When the neighbors complained and refused to allow their children to play with Butch, his father grounded him.   Nevertheless, Butch continued to threaten other children, especially Stewart S. After this last incident on the bus, Butch came home with a pocketful of school supplies that he took from Stewart's book bag.

1. Identify the behaviors that concern you in this case. What developmental problem do these behaviors suggest?

_____

_____

_____

Using Bibliotherapy in Developmental Counseling

Bibliotherapy is a counseling technique that can help children overcome common developmental problems such as those described in Chapter 2. Common developmental problems can be associated with attachment and dependency; fear and its related responses, which include shyness, embarrassment, worry, and anxiety; and anger and its related responses of aggression and jealousy. The two case studies profiled in this chapter of the manual illustrate how a timid child like Stewart may not be assertive enough to deal with Butch, an overly aggressive child who bullies his way through life.

The author has selected *The Mouse, the Monster and Me: Assertiveness for Young People* by Pat Palmer (see Media Suggestions) to help children like Stewart and Butch learn new ways of thinking and behaving. This book, which can be used with small and large groups, is designed to help children understand that "mouse" types are sometimes so nice that they allow others to make decisions that they should make. On the other hand, "monsters" are usually not friendly or nice and confuse inner strength with "acting tough." This book is full of games and activities to help children learn about themselves and to practice acting less like a "mouse" or like a "monster." It is a book designed to help all children use their inner strength or "power" to take charge of their own lives.

Suggested Supplemental Activities

1. Provide the children with puppets that represent the "mouse" and the "monster" and ask them to create a series of puppet plays. Ask the children to identify some common characteristics of the mouse (e.g., timid, afraid) and of the monster (e.g., bully, aggressive).

2. Initiate a discussion about children's rights and responsibilities. What are some ways to assert your rights without being a "mouse" or a "monster"?

3. Role play scenarios in which : a) someone who used to be a "mouse" stands up for him or herself, or b) a "monster" learns to be more thoughtful and friendly.

Media Suggestions

Books

Palmer, P. (1977). *The mouse, the monster and me: Assertiveness for young people.* San Luis Obispo, CA: Impact Publishers.

This book, now in its eleventh printing, is full of ideas about how to help children learn more about themselves, be assertive and make good decisions. It provides helpful exercises on how to help children recognize their strengths and special qualities. By building self-esteem, it helps children assert their rights and enables them to be themselves rather than a "mouse" or "monster." Ideal for individual and group sessions with all children.

Pardeck, J. T. & Pardeck, J. A. (1993). *Bibliotherapy: A Clinical Approach for Helping Children*. Landhorne, PA: Gordon & Breach Science Publishers.

The bibliotherapeutic approach, a helping strategy that can be used to assist children with crisis situations, clinical problems and developmental concerns, is described in this book. In addition, the authors provide a synopsis of numerous children's books that address a variety of childhood problems.

Pardeck, J.A. & Pardeck, J.T. (1986). *Books for early childhood: A Developmental Perspective*.   New York: Greenwood Press.

This is a compilation of children's literature that can be used to help youngsters cope with developmental change. Each section suggests books that can be used to help children cope with common development needs.   It provides titles designed to help children address concerns associated with anger, attitudes and values, family relationships, fear and fantasy, motor development and physical change, peers and school, self-image and sex roles, single-parent and blended families and special developmental needs.

Palmer, P. (1977). *The mouse, the monster and me: Assertiveness for young people.* San Luis Obispo, CA: Impact Publishers.

This book, now in its eleventh printing, is full of ideas about how to help children learn more about themselves, be assertive, and make good decisions. It provides helpful exercises on how to help children recognize their strengths and special qualities. By building self-esteem, it helps children assert their rights and enables them to be themselves rather than a "mouse" or "monster." Ideal for individual and group sessions with all children.

Chapter 9
Behavioral Approaches with Children

This chapter explores the theoretical and practical aspects of behavioral therapy, which is one of the major counseling approaches being utilized today with children. Principles of behavioral therapy included in this chapter are positive and negative reinforcement; punishment, and response cost. Treatment planning is discussed as it relates to behavioral therapy, particularly in the areas of A-B-C assessment, deficit and excess behaviors, and treatment goals. The role of evaluation regarding treatment strategies is also included.

Learning Objectives

Upon completion of this chapter, you will be able to:

1. List and describe the principles of operant conditioning.

2. Discuss the goal and rational of the treatment plan.

3. List and describe treatment strategies.

4. Explain reasons behavioral therapy programs may fail.

5. Describe the purpose and method of evaluation of the treatment plan.

Review Exercises

1. Define behavioral therapy.

2. What are some problems exhibited by children who may benefit from behavioral therapy?

3. What is efficacy research? What is its significance in behavioral therapy?

4. List and describe the four general principles of operant conditioning.

5. Describe the principles of cognitive-behavioral therapy (CBT).

6. What is the goal of treatment in behavioral therapy? What is the "key feature"?

7. What is A-B-C analysis?

8. Define deficit behavior. List the procedures that increase deficit behavior.

9. What strategies or procedures are used to eliminate excess or undesired behavior?

10. How are treatment goals evaluated?

11. What does "systematic and objective" evaluation include?

Awareness Exercises

1. What is your general feeling about behavioral therapy? Do you like it? Do you think it is useful in changing behavior in the long term? Why? Why not?

2. In this chapter, the following statement appears under the section on Planning Treatment: "It is important to note that not all behavior can be altered; nor do most advocates of behavioral therapy adhere to the view that all behavior is learned." Do you agree or disagree? Defend and explain your response.

3. Would you, in the role of the counselor, be comfortable using behavioral therapy strategies? Why? Why not?

4. Can you (if you are not an only child) remember instances of sibling rivalry in your childhood? How did your parents or other caregivers manage this? Can you think of specific examples? Are there any aspects of behavioral therapy strategies in the approaches used? (If you have children, answer these questions by evaluating your managing of the conflicts or rivalries between your children.) What behaviors in your own childhood (or those of your children) were increased or decreased as a potential result of the way in which these conflicts were managed?

Practical Applications

" Go Ahead, Hit Me! You Can't Hurt Steel"
The Case of Jorge F.

Jeorge F. is the youngest of three children. His parents are divorced and he lives with his mother, his 12-year-old brother, Ramon and his sister, Lily, an 18-year-old college freshman. Jorge annoys his older brother and continually provokes him by saying, " Go ahead and hit me! You can't hurt steel!" Although Ramon can sometimes keep Jorge's attention by playing a game with him, a physical fight usually breaks out between the two brothers. A confrontation is more likely if Ramon responds to Jorge's challenge by arguing back. By contrast, Jorge usually behaves when left in the sole care of his sister Lily, whom he likes and admires.

Since his parents' divorce, Jorge has been in constant conflict with his mother who has tried to take over the role of disciplinarian. This continual antagonism is a great strain on Jorge's mother who is always struggling with him to do necessary daily tasks such as getting ready for school. Mrs. F. has been hospitalized for depression within the last year and attributes her emotional problems to the enormous amounts of stress associated with supporting the family and coping with Jorge's behavior.

Jorge usually spends two nights a week with his dad. During these visits, Mr. F. never misses a chance to criticize Mrs. F. He tells Jorge that his mother is not trying to help him and does not care about him. Mr. F.'s way of handling Jorge is to let him do exactly as he pleases. In this way, he avoids conflict with his son. Occasionally, however, Mr. F. will bring Jorge home early because he is "acting up" and will exclaim "I need a break!" Sometimes, Jorge's dad refuses to take Jorge for his weekly visits and invites Ramon instead. When he does take Jorge, Mr. F. works on horse racing forms while Jorge plays video games late into the night.

At home, Jorge seems to be able to "tune out" his mother's requests and/or reprimands and has little regard for her feelings. He occasionally "breaks" her precious possessions and those of his brother, Ramon. However, he has never deliberately ruined anything that belonged to Lily or himself. Lately, he has become very violent when he is forced to do something that he does not want to do. He has hit his mother on several occasions when she tried to punish him for fighting or destroying the property of others.

Jorge's attention can be sustained by a number of activities that capture his interest. For example, he can play a lengthy game of chess with his brother or watch an hour-long television program that he enjoys. However, at school, Jorge's teacher note that Jorge is constantly out of his seat and can't concentrate on any one thing for very long. He has to be continually reminded to finish his work and is always being reprimanded. Although these problems have always been present, they have intensified since his parents' divorce.

Friendless, Jorge is always arguing and getting into fistfights with his peers. Because of his disruptive behavior, Jorge has been expelled from the private grade school he has attended for five years, and he will be placed in an alternative educational setting for 5th grade. Specific behavior problems noted on his psychological evaluation and referral include noncompliance, physical aggression toward peers, attention-seeking behavior, tantrums, and a high activity level.

Behavioral Assessment and Treatment Plan

Generally, children who are struggling with a variety of *real-life* problems will display a number of troublesome behaviors that do not necessarily fit neatly into a particular DSM-IV category. Therefore, children, who have not read the textbooks and do not know which symptoms they are entitled to, may **not** present a "textbook" list of behaviors that can be easily identified. This is particularly true in the case of Jorge, who has been diagnosed with Attention Deficit Hyperactivity Disorder (ADHD) by one physician and with Oppositional Defiant Disorder (ODD) by another. Each prescribed different medications: the first recommended Dexadrine (Dextroamphetamine); the second suggested a trial on Prozac (Flouxetine). Currently, Jorge takes 10 milligrams of Prozac daily.

Medication has met with minimal success, and a plan of intervention is needed that will help Jorge change his maladaptive behavior. The following exercises are designed to assist the counselor in developing an active treatment plan for Jorge that includes participation by his family. Specific exercises provide practice in completing an A-B-C assessment, defining treatment goals, and selecting behavioral strategies and activities that can be used as specific interventions.

A-B-C Assessment

1. Complete an A-B-C analysis of Jorge's behavior.

Trigger

Antecedents (A) refer to stimuli occurring prior to the behavior in question. *limits are set*

parents divorce

annoys + provokes his older brother

Visits with Dad with minimal supervision

Hearing his mother is does not care about him

Behavior (B) is defined in observable terms

fights   *breaking items*

can't concentrate at school

constant conflict with mother

Consequences (C) represent the events that follow the behavior.

expelled from school

has no friends

2. Do arguing and fighting pay off for Jorge? If so, explain how.

No

Treatment Goals

3. Formulate a number of terminal treatment goals for Jorge and his family. These treatment goals should be stated in broad behavioral terms (e.g., Jorge will learn to *increase* the use of compromise *decrease* the use of aggression in handling disagreements).

Treatment Goal #1

To have less than 2 physical fights by end of 3 wks.

Treatment Goal #2

To remain seated at least 85% of class time

Treatment Goal #3

Have no more than one argument with brothers per day for one week

Treatment Goal #4 (include parents and siblings)

Be 80% compliant with mother's discipline within 2 wks.

Treatment Strategies

4. Treatment <u>strategies</u> should be specific behavioral techniques (e.g., positive reinforcement, time out, behavioral rehearsal) used to increase or decrease designated actions. Describe the intermediate behavioral strategies that you will use to accomplish each terminal treatment goal.

Strategies to achieve treatment goal #1 include:

Improve conflict resolution through role playing w/ therapist
Self imposed time out

Strategies to achieve treatment goal #2 include:

over

Practice imagery of playing video games to stay seated
Compliant with meds

Strategies to achieve treatment goal # 3 include:

Impose of time out, count to 10, deep breathing, self-
talk.

Strategies to achieve treatment goal # 4 include:

_____

_____

5. According to Dr. Phelps, the author of chapter 9, it is "far better to teach, model, and reinforce a desired behavior than to try to eliminate an undesired behavior." Do you agree with Dr. Phelp's statement? If so, describe how teaching, modeling and positive reinforcement of desired behavior can be applied to Jorge's behavior problems.

_____

_____

_____

Media Suggestions

Books

Kaplan, J.S. with Carter, J. (1995). *Beyond Behavior Modification: A Cognitive-Behavioral Approach to Behavior Management in the School.* (3rd. ed). Austin, TX: Pro-Ed.

This text focuses on behavior-management strategies that include both traditional behavior modification and social learning theory. Each strategy is presented in a simple easy-to-understand style that will assist students, teachers, and counseling professionals who want to learn more about behavior management.

Kaplan, J.S., with Wald, M.G. (1996). *Kid Mod: Empowering Children and Youth Through Instruction in the Use of Reinforcement Principles.* Austin, TX: Pro-Ed.

Kid Mod is designed to teach children, ranging in age from 9 through 12- the theory and practice of reinforcement principles. Students learn how to use positive reinforcement and extinction to change own behavior. Children learn how to get what they want from themselves and others without resorting to antisocial and counterproductive behaviors. An audiocassette is also available.

Videos

Breathing Away Stress. FH: Films for the Humanities and Sciences, P.O. Box 2053, Princeton, NJ 08543-2053.

Eli Bay leads the class in a series of deep-breathing exercises designed to manage stress and promote relaxation. Students learn breathing and massage to release emotions causing stress. (30 minutes, color)

Walking Through the Storm (1990). Insight Media, 2162 Broadway, New York, NY 10024.

Part I. *Working with Aggressive Children and Youth* combines scenes of children acting out their   feelings of confusion, anger and alienation with explanations from psychologists on managing aggressive behavior. (45 minutes)

Part II. *Strategies for Responding* illustrates interventions that help aggressive children reorient their behavior. Viewers see how modeling and verbal input can help children decrease internal stress and conflict. Conflict Cycle, Life Space Interview, and Guided Group Interaction are the three models for managing behavior presented in the video. (45 minutes)

Chapter 10
Safeguarding Children's Rights

All aspects of children's rights are addressed in this chapter. Children's rights in therapy as related to consent, feedback, privacy, and confidentiality are examined. Potential risks to children's rights are also presented regarding documentation, taping, computerized storage and third-party disclosures. Legal and ethical issues are identified and consequences of violations discussed.

Learning Objectives

Upon completing this chapter, you will be able to:

1. Describe and discuss the rights of the child in counseling.

2. List and describe the potential risks to children's rights.

3. Describe the ethical issues related to the counseling of children.

4. Describe the legal issues related to the counseling of children.

5. Explain the ethical and legal responsibilities of child counselors inherent in the duty to warn and protect and the duty to report child abuse.

6. Describe the necessary steps in making a report of suspected child abuse.

Review Exercises

1. Describe the events in the evolution of children's rights culminating in the recognition of the child as a person.

2. List the rights agreed upon at the 1989 UN Convention on the Rights of Children as summarized by Wilcox and Naimark.

3. Which of the rights granted to children at the 1989 UN Convention relate to the dignity of the child; to the child's right to protection and treatment; and to the child's right to self-determination?

4. List and explain three important reasons therapy with children presents a special challenge to mental health counselors.

5. What is the child therapist's "primary responsibility"? What are some obstacles to fulfilling this responsibility?

6. Define and describe informed consent.

7. What aspects of counseling services do the parents of the child need to understand before counseling begins?

8. Who gets "feedback" in child counseling? Why?

9. List three ways in which the counselor can protect the child's right to privacy.

10. Who is protected under the "child-therapist" privilege? In what instances can this be claimed or waived? When can confidentiality be breached?

11. List and discuss the four areas in which children's rights are most likely to be at risk.

12. List the set of values that, according to Blocher (1987), govern counseling practice.

13. What duty does the counselor have to "warn and protect" if a client poses a clear and imminent danger to self and/or others? Identify some ways to protect the child and the therapist when the "duty to warn" is invoked.

14. According to David Sandberg, (Sandberg, Crabbs, & Crabbs, 1988), what three conditions are **not** necessary for a child abuse report to be filed?

15. List the thirteen common signs of abuse and neglect.

Awareness Exercises

1. Melton said that "prevention should be the cornerstone of child mental health policy." What is your assessment of government and society's participation in adopting preventive practices and policies? Do you judge these to be adequate or inadequate? Why? Why not?

2. Read the *Hippocratic Oath* included in the section on "Children's Rights in Therapy" in this chapter. Can you think of any obstacles, challenges, and/or problems that may occur (other than those noted in this chapter) in fulfilling the responsibility of this oath?

3. Read the informed consent forms for the child and the parents and/or guardians that are presented in Appendix 2. Do you think you would have any difficulty presenting the informed consent form to child and/or the parent? Are you uncomfortable with any of the content? Why? Why not?

4. In the section entitled "Legal and Ethical Guidelines for Practitioners, "a statement is made: "There is general agreement that counselors should understand their own value systems in order to be effective in fulfilling their responsibilities to their clients, to their individual professions and to the welfare of society." Write about your own value system. What are the cornerstones? Compare your values to the set of values presented by Blocher (1987) in the section cited above.

5. Do you know of or have you ever known an "abused child"? Is the list of common signs of abuse and neglect consistent with the example that you have in mind? Write about your feelings regarding the victims of child abuse and the perpetrators. Do you think these feelings will help or hinder your ability to counsel abused and neglected children?

Practical Applications

The Duty to Report
" I Fall a Lot ": The Case of Julie L.

Julie is eight years old and is in the third grade. She is small and frail and looks younger than her age. She has two front teeth missing. Julie has an older sister who is 11 and a younger brother who is five. Mr. L. is a traveling salesman for a pharmaceutical firm and is away from home for several days at a time. Mrs. L. doesn't work outside of the home. When her husband is away she is often confined to the house for days at a time because the family has only one car. Mrs. L. is the primary disciplinarian in the family because her husband is away so much of the time. She sets high standards for her children and expects them to be able to make decisions on their own.

Ms. B., the third-grade teacher, says that Julie is a very quiet girl who does well in school but does not get involved in many activities. She notes that Julie often comes to school with bruises, bumps, or a large band-aid covering a part of an arm or a leg. When asked about her injuries, Julie either says nothing or explains that she "fell." Mrs. L. attends PTA regularly and is such a nice person that Ms. B. doesn't think that she is responsible for the child's injuries.

Last week, Julie came to school with an ace bandage around her arm. When the counselor was reading to Julie, she noticed that Julie seemed to be in pain. Although Julie would not say how her arm was injured, the counselor suggested that the nurse might be able to help her feel better. Together they walked to the nurse's office.

When the nurse examined Julie, she found numerous bruises and lacerations on the child's back and arms. The nurse noticed swollen areas where the skin was broken and bleeding slightly. L-shaped welts, similar to those caused by the edge of the belt buckle that had broken the skin, appeared on Julie's back in several places. The nurse suspected that Julie had been beaten with a belt.

1. What should be done immediately?

_____

_____

_____

_____

2. What is the procedure for reporting child abuse in your state?

_____

_____

_____

_____

3. What needs to be done to help Julie and her family?

_____

_____

_____

_____

REPORTING CHILD ABUSE AND NEGLECT *

Who are mandated reporters?

"Persons who, in the course of their employment, occupation or practice of their profession come into contact with children shall report or cause a report to me made...when they have reasonable cause to suspect on the basis of their medical, professional or other training and experience, that a child coming before them in their professional or official capacity is an abused child. Except with respect to confidential communications made to an ordained member of the clergy . . ., the privileged communication between any professional person shall not apply to situations involving child abuse and shall not constitute grounds for failure to report."

Immunity from Liability

"A person, hospital, institution, school facility, agency or agency employee that participates in good faith in making a report, cooperating with an investigation, testifying in a proceeding arising out of an instance of suspected child abuse, the taking of photographs or the removal or keeping of a child (in protective custody). . ., shall have immunity from civil and   criminal, that might otherwise result by reason of those actions. . ."

Penalties for Failure to Report

"A person or official required to report a case of suspected child abuse who willfully fails to do so commits a summary offense for the first violation and a misdemeanor of the third degree fora second and subsequent violation."

---

* The information on reporting in this section is quoted from Chapter 63 of the Child Protection Services Law, PA ACT 124 of 1975, as amended by Act l0 (SS1) of 1995.

INSTRUCTION FOR REPORTING

Reports from persons required to report suspected child abuse shall be made immediately by telephone and in writing within 48 hours after the <u>oral report.</u>

<u>Written reports</u> shall include the following information if available:

1. The names and addresses of the child and the parents or other person responsible for the care of the child if known.

2. Where the suspected abuse occurred.

3. The age and sex of the subjects of the report.

4. The nature and extent of the suspected child abuse including any evidence of prior abuse to the child or siblings of the child.

5. The name and relationship of the person or persons responsible for causing the suspected abuse, if known, and any evidence of prior abuse by that person or persons.

6. Family composition.

7. The source of the report.

8. The person making the report and where that person can be reached.

9. The actions taken by the reporting source, including the taking of photographs and X-rays, removal or keeping of the child or notifying the medical examiner or coroner.

10. Any other information which the department may require by regulation.

Media Suggestions

Books

Besharov, D.J. (1985). *The Vulnerable Social Worker: Liability for Serving Children and Families.* Annapolis, MD: NASW.

Written by a lawyer, this book covers liability insurance, Legal Defense Services, professional standards, and the grievance process. An excellent reference for legal liability, this is a resource book on how to practice child welfare.

Goodman, E. & Bottoms, B.L. (Eds.). (1993). *Child victims, child witnesses: Understanding and improving testimony.* New York: Guilford Press.

This book, which offers a discussion of the latest child witness research, is a must read for mental health, social service, medical and legal professionals. Especially helpful to practitioners are the chapters on using anatomically correct dolls for evaluating child sexual abuse, improving children's testimony with preparation and hearing and testing children's evidence.

Hillman, D. & Solek-Tefft, J. (1988). *Spiders and Flies: Help for parents and teachers of sexually abused children.* Lexington, MA.: D.C. Heath.

This book offers parents, teachers, and counselors critical information on how to help children and their families with the *aftermath* of reported child sexual abuse. Chapter 11 gives valuable information for helping the child cope with the many and varied aspects of the legal process.

Sandberg, D., Crabbs, S.K. & Crabbs, M.A. (1988, April). Legal issues in child abuse: Questions and answers for counselors. *Elementary School Guidance & Counseling, 22,* 268-274.

David Sandberg, an attorney who specializes in children's issues, answers questions that counselors frequently ask about reporting child abuse.

Videos

Child Abuse: It Shouldn't Hurt to Be a Kid (1985). Insight Media, 2162 Broadway, New
York, NY. 10024.

In this video, all mandated reporters (e.g., mental health professionals, educators,
social-service employees, and day care providers) are advised of their responsibilities
under the law. It defines child abuse, teaches how to recognize it, and explains where to
report suspected abuse. (27 minutes).

Childhood Sexual Abuse. FH: Films for the Humanities and Sciences, P.O. Box 2053,
Princeton, NJ 08543-2053.

In this video, psychiatrists, social workers, and law enforcement officials explain
how the pattern of abuse spreads throughout the family, why children can be manipulated
into silent acceptance of abuse, the signs of sexual abuse, and how and to whom it should
be reported.

Classrooms, Courtrooms and Common Sense. (1991). Insight Media, 2162 Broadway,
New York, NY. 10024.

This series on administrative liability helps school staff understand what actions
can lead to a lawsuit. It distinguishes between civil and criminal suits and explains
negligence and intentional torts. An attorney uses on-site simulations to explain school
law.

Confidentiality. (1983). Insight Media, 2162 Broadway, New York, NY. 10024.

This video aids therapists in matters related to maintaining confidentiality. It
presents vignettes of situations in which confidentiality issues may arise and examines the
types of responses that are appropriate when confidential information is requested.

Documentation: Your Best Defense. (1992). Insight Media, 2162 Broadway, New York,
NY 10024.

The therapist is taught the important aspects of constructing a good report. This
includes analyzing the situation and understanding what to report and how to report it.(40
min.)

Chapter 11
Parents as Partners in Child Counseling

An Adlerian approach to understanding the child's misbehavior introduces this chapter and serves as a backdrop for discussing the child's place in the family and his or her struggle for love, approval, and acceptance. The value of making parents partners in the counseling process -- for the child, parent and counselor-- is presented. This partnership is related to the counseling process which includes its stages, techniques, and special issues.

Learning Objectives

Upon completing this chapter, you will be able to:

1. List and discuss the goals of the child's misbehavior. Discuss the Adlerian approach to understanding all behavior.

2. Define and describe the purposes of parent counseling.

3. Discuss the value of counseling with parents.

4. Identify the various types of parenting styles and discuss potential effects.

5. Describe the counseling process, its stages, and its techniques.

6. Characterize the special issues related to the counseling process.

Review Exercises

1. Explain Adlerian theory regarding behavior presented in this chapter. Specifically, define *striving for significance; feelings of inferiority*; and *lifestyle.*

2. List and describe the four goals of misbehavior.

3. How does the family's style of coping with life influence whether the child will take a positive or negative path toward development?

4. Characterize the following family atmospheres: authoritarian, suppressive, rejective, disparaging, high standards, inharmonious, inconsistent, materialistic, over-protective, pitying, hopeless, martyr, and "parent becomes peer."

5. Define parent counseling. What purposes does parent counseling serve?

6. What five things are parents enabled to do through their involvement in the counseling process?

7. List and describe the four phases of the Adlerian counseling process.

8. Define and discuss the interpersonal dimensions of the helping relationship as defined by Carl Rogers.

9. List and describe the reasons parents are often apprehensive about consulting with teachers, counselors, and other school personnel.

10. What is the value of obtaining background information, and information pertaining to the child's school performance and behavior, in the counseling process involving parents?

11. What are the five component parts of the model for counseling with parents individually presented in this chapter?

12. How can the counselor determine what the child's goals are for misbehavior? What content in the parents' perception of the child is significant?

Awareness Exercises

1. The introduction of this chapter describes the many roles parents are expected to fill in child- rearing and states that the responsibility of these roles would "present a Herculean challenge to a team of professionals." What are your feelings about what is expected of parents? Too much? Too little? Are you sympathetic with the statement? What implications does this statement have for you as a counselor?

2. Of the four types of misbehavior discussed in this chapter, which do you think you would find the most troublesome to deal with? Why? Elaborate.

3. According to Mosak and Dreikurs, each child looks for his or her own "place in the sun" within the family constellation. "One child may fit in by being the best and another by being the worst" (Kern & Carlson, 1981, p. 303). After rereading the section on "The Child's Place in the Family," how do you think that you found your "place in the sun" in your family? What role do you think that you played? How do you feel about it in retrospect?

4. Reread the section on the family atmosphere. Are there any aspects of the negative parenting styles described that fit your own experiences of being parented or of parenting? What do you think were the effects (behavior patterns or attitudes) on you or on your children?

5. The introduction to "Parents as Partners in Child Counseling" includes the statement: " All parents make mistakes because they are human." Are you forgiving or sympathetic toward your own parents (or toward yourself if you are a parent)? Why does the author make this statement? Does she seem to value understanding and empathy for parents? Do you share the author's perspective?

Practical Applications

I Didn't Have a Clue About How to Parent a Child"
The Case of Trevor T.

Background Information

Eight-year-old Trevor lives with his sister, brother, mother, and mother's paramour. Trevor, described by his mother as a "sickly" child, is the middle child in his family. His older sister, Shawna, is a very mature and outgoing 11 year old, and his younger brother, Charley, described as quiet and shy, just turned 6. Shawna has a special bond with Charley because she helped care for him during her mother's many illnesses and hospitalizations. Whenever Charley is feeling hurt or insecure, he turns to Shawna to get the extra attention he needs. Trevor and Charley generally get along despite episodes of intense sibling rivalry. They share a bedroom and spend the majority of their time playing together after school and on weekends. All of the children worry about their mother's health problems and are very protective of her.

Shawna was born when Ms. T. was 16 years old and unmarried. Trevor's father, who reportedly abused Ms. T. and the children, is no longer living with the family. Although Shawna has no contact with her biological father, the boys are "required" to visit their father, who retains visitation rights. According to Ms. T, all of the children get along with her live-in boyfriend and call him "Dad."

In discussing her own childhood, Ms. T. revealed a long history of both physical and sexual abuse at the hands of her alcoholic father. Her mother, also an alcoholic, did not intervene to help her. Ms. T. says she took her father's abuse "to make things easier for my mother." Like Trevor, Ms. T. was a middle child who says she was the "scapegoat" of her family. As a child and adolescent, she had frequent stays in a number of foster homes. Ms. T is candid about her lack of parenting skills and says; " I didn't have a clue about how to parent a child." Despite being raised in a dysfunctional family, Ms. T desperately wants her children to have a normal home life, one that she never had.

Trevor T. came into the world as a full-term baby who weighed 8 lbs 14 oz. He had some jaundice after birth but went home from the hospital with his mother. Ms. T. reports that little Trevor was about two weeks old when he stopped breathing. This episode was the first of five such attacks during infancy. Between the ages of 7 months and 2 years, Trevor underwent a series of tests and was diagnosed with severe asthma.

According to his mother, Trevor wasn't speaking at age 2. He couldn't say "mama" and would only utter sounds such as "ooh" or "augh" or he would scream. His motor and language skills were slow to develop and his mother blames this on his many hospitalizations. She recalls that Trevor regressed during hospital stays and had to be diapered and bottle fed. He was almost 4 years old before he was toilet trained.

During his second year, Trevor got a new baby brother, Charley, who was born prematurely. Charley was also diagnosed with asthma and both brothers spent a great deal of time in hospitals. After Charley was born, Trevor was hospitalized for breathing problems five (5) times in a 30-day period. The frequency of his hospitalizations prompted a report of suspected child abuse and neglect and an investigation by Children's Services followed. It was through this agency that Ms. T. asked for and received help with parenting.

When Trevor was 3, his mother was hospitalized a second time for depression. She had been coping with two children who were, according to her, constantly sick and in need of in-patient hospitalization. She began to request medication that would sedate the boys so that she could sleep. According to Ms. T., the boys were up continually through the night and she, unable to sleep, collapsed and was hospitalized for 28 days. The children were again placed in foster care. Trevor was in his new foster home for only two days when his foster mother called to say that she "couldn't handle him because of the medication schedule."

Trevor appears to be an average second grader, although school is not his favorite past-time. He receives mostly C's on his report card and expresses a dislike for reading. His behavior in school, as described by his teachers, is passive, obedient, and polite, sometimes bordering on rigid. According the school psychologist who evaluated him, Trevor "worries" a great deal about his mother and her health and seems very concerned about his own health problems. Although his behavior continues to be a significant problem at home, Trevor's behavior in the structured school environment is acceptable and does not appear to warrant intervention at this time.

Trevor was brought to play therapy by his mother because of his behavior at home. According to his mother, he can't sit still, won't listen, and is very aggressive toward his brother, sister, and mother. His mother, in the initial interview, described him as " a bully to other people, but inside he is very sensitive and very afraid." The mother also noted that he has mood swings (similar to her own) and that he appears to be "depressed." She thinks his moodiness may be a side-effect of the medicine that he takes to prevent seizures.

Trevor's drawings, done in the first session, provided themes of Trevor, his brother, and sister hurting one another and Trevor hurting himself. He commented that he did not like his brother, sister or his mother's boyfriend but would not elaborate. He got very emotional while talking about his mother's medical problems and said, "Her dad and my dad beat her up. . .a lot."

During Trevor's individual play session he enjoyed having absolute freedom-- no controls, no discipline, and no lectures. Frequently, in sociodramatic play, he would "criticize" the therapist. For example, as the therapist was washing the make-believe dishes, Trevor instructed her that she was washing them "wrong, " and stacking them "wrong" and he showed her how to do dishes correctly. In another session, Trevor had to leave to do "cop" work and the therapist was to do the dishes and put them away while he was gone. When he came home, he told the therapist that she had not put them away "correctly" and so he did the dishes. He collected all of the dishes in a pail, added liquid soap to the water, and thoroughly enjoyed mixing and messing.

Mutual parent and therapist goals for Trevor's involvement in play therapy were: a) improved interpersonal interaction, b) development of self-confidence, and c) increased ability to express his feelings. One-on-one sessions with the play therapist were followed by a group play therapy session which included Trevor, his siblings and his mother as well as other children and their parents. During one play group session, Trevor was actively involved in a group game and his mother told him " You better rest. You're going to have an asthma attack!" He obeyed his mother and sat down-- quiet and alone. Although no signs of asthmatic breathing were evident, Ms. T. was convinced an attack was imminent, and Trevor was visibly afraid of getting sick.

The therapist's general impression is that Trevor is a kind and sensitive youngster who has been taught right from wrong, sometimes to the point of rigidity. His mother is sometimes overprotective, causing Trevor to doubt his own thoughts and decisions. This overprotection is most likely the result of Trevor's many illnesses. Ms. T. is a survivor and is teaching her children to be survivors as well. Her strength as a single-parent is admirable and her need to be strict is understood. However, Ms. T's overly critical attitude toward Trevor has afforded few opportunities for him to grow in self-confidence and independence. Nevertheless, Ms. T is trying to be a good mother and has taken positive steps to improve her parenting skills. Recognizing and building on these strengths, Ms. T. needs encouragement to improve her relationship with her son.

" I Didn't Have a Clue About How to Parent a Child":
Session with Trevor's Mother

The following model for counseling with parents individually is illustrated and explained in the text. This model is applicable to all parents, not just parents of children who are having problems. It can be used to develop or strengthen the parent-child relationship in preventive, developmental, or remedial counseling in school, private practice, clinic, or agency settings.

1. **Solicit information from the parent to determine his/her concept of the child.**

2. **Obtain an expression of the parent's feeling toward the child.**

3. **Help the parent explore the parent-child relationship.**

4. **Assist the parent understand and empathize with the child.**

5. **Help the parent emphasize the positive aspects of the child's personality.**

6. **Encourage the parent to formulate ways to improve and strengthen the parent-child relationship.**

Determine the Parent's Concept of the Child

Ms. T. : Trevor is a bully, but then he is a big baby at the same time. You yell at him and he doesn't get tears. Instead, he just flies off the handle. Little things that wouldn't normally   bother a person will bother him. I know that is how I was when I was young.

Counselor:

_____

_____

_____

Ms. T.: Trevor is a lot like me.........stubborn.   He will *deliberately* do things just to get a rise out of me!

Counselor:

_____

_____

_____

Ms. T: I'd say that Trevor needs extra attention. . . because of his illness. I try not to bring it up, but I am very worried about it. I try to make light of his problems.

_____

_____

_____

Obtain an Expression of the Parent's Feeling Toward the Child

Ms. T.:   I tell you honestly that there were times when I wanted to walk out the door and never come back. Many, many times. . . but I held on because I love my kids. You know, to me they always come first. It scares me at times when I have these feelings of anger toward them.

Counselor:

_____

_____

_____

Ms. T.:   I don't abuse my children. Of course, there are times when I'd love to throw them through a wall, but. . .

Counselor:

_____

_____

_____

Help the Parent Explore the Parent-Child Relationship

Ms. T.: Before I was hospitalized, I told the caseworker; "I'm afraid. I'm scared to death that I'm going to hurt my kids. Help me."

Counselor:

_____

_____

_____

Ms. T.: I took parenting classes because I told them that I didn't know how to show love to my child. I know I love Trevor, but how do I let him know it?

Counselor:.

_____

_____

_____

Ms. T.: Maybe Tommy feels neglected. . .Shawna talks to him and Trevor is able to open up to her. Shawna and I can sit and talk about anything. Charley and I can talk about anything, but Trevor is more like I was. Very quiet and withdrawn. I was very sensitive. I escaped into books and daydreaming and so does he.

Counselor:

_____

_____

_____

Assist the Parent to Understand and Empathize with the Child

Ms. T.:   I was the middle child and I felt neglected. I was the one who was picked on the most.

Counselor:

_____

_____

_____

Ms. T.:   I have been in several foster homes. I was five-years-old when my father beat me so bad that the neighbors called the cops. That was the first time I was taken away.

Counselor:

_____

_____

_____

Ms. T.:   I find myself sitting and looking at my son and saying, " Hey, wait a minute. What are you saying to your son? Stop! You sound like your father."

Counselor:

_____

_____

_____

Help the Parent to Emphasize the Positive Aspects of the Child's Personality

Ms. T.:   All of my kids, including Trevor, know what is expected of them. . . They take their turn doing dishes and other chores --.they don't always do them right.-- but they are learning.

Counselor:

_____

_____

_____

Ms. T.:   It is hard to think about Trevor's good points. He is between Shawna, who does everything right, and Charley, who is this sweet little kid who can do no wrong. And then there is Trevor in the middle.

Counselor:

_____

_____

_____

Ms. T: When I was growing up, I felt like the ugly ducking between two swans. I wanted so much for people to notice me and to approve of me. I wonder if Trevor is feeling like I did: "Can't do anything right, so why try?"

Counselor:

_____

_____

_____

Encourage the Parent to Formulate Ways to Improve and Strengthen the Parent-Child Relationship

Ms. T.: Sometimes, I see myself in Trevor. He is sensitive and worries a lot like I did when I was a kid. I never felt I could tell my mother anything because she just couldn't handle it.

Counselor:

_____

_____

_____

Ms. T.: I tell him, "I am your mother and I love you. I want you to be able to talk to me and if you have done something wrong, you can tell me and we will talk about it." But he doesn't.

Counselor:

_____

_____

_____

Ms. T.: One day Trevor said, "You don't love me like you love Charley. You love Charley more". I said, "No, you are wrong. I love each of you the same , but in different ways."

Counselor:

_____

_____

_____

Media Suggestions

Books

Bratton, M. (1987).   *A Guide to Family Intervention.*   Pompano Beach, FL: Health Communications.

This guide offers a step-by-step process for confronting the alcoholic or chemically dependent person with the problem of his or her addiction. It deals with family fears and denial while encouraging the open discussion of difficult subjects.

Faber, A. & Mazlish, E. (1980). *How to Talk So Kids Will Listen. How to Listen So Kids Will Talk.* New York: Rawson Wade Publishers.

This best-selling book offers innovative ways to solve common problems in the parent-child relationship. It is filled with cartoons, anecdotes and the authors' own experiences.

Glenn, H. S. & Nelson, J. (1989). *Raising Self-Reliant Children.* Rocklin, LA:: Prima Publications.

The authors offer an original and lucid explanation of why so many of our young people are failing to feel capable and responsible. The authors show how today's parents, through their desire to indulge children materially, fail to make them feel that they are a contributing part of the family.

Main, F. (1986). *Perfect Parenting and Other Myths.*   Minneapolis, MN: CompCare Publications.

The Flawless Father and Magical Mother are myths according to this author. He tells parents to relax and let go of unrealistic expectations about being a perfect parent.

McElroy, E. (Ed.). (1988). *Children and Adolescents with Mental Illness: A Parents' Guide*. Kensington, MD: Woodbine House.

Deals realistically with problems parents face when mental illness strikes a child. The book provides guidance about therapists, hospitals, crises and emergencies, the educational and legal rights of children and planning for the future. Encourages parents to learn about mental illness and be assertive in treatment decisions.

Nelsen, J. (1987). *Positive Discipline.* New York: Ballantine Books.

A warm, practical, step-by step sourcebook for parents and teachers. Learn how to encourage self-respect, self-discipline, cooperation, good behavior and problem-solving skills in children.

Schaefer, C. (1984). *How to Talk to Your Children About Really Important Things*. New York: Harper & Row.

For parents of 5 to 12-year-old children, this book covers the when, why and how of talking with youngsters. Regardless of the subject, you can learn how to become an "askable" parent.

Sharmat, M. (1984). *My Mother Never Listens to Me.* Niles, IL: Albert Whitman.

Young readers will empathize with Jerome's problem, while adults will appreciate his mother's situation. This book is best read together.

Simon, N. (1983). *I Wish I Had My Father.* Niles, IL: A Whitman.

Young children will look at the pictures and relate to the problem, "I hate Father's Day." This read-aloud book offers mother and child a chance to talk about sad feelings.

Simon, N. (1981). *Nobody's Perfect, Not Even My Mother.* Niles, IL: Albert Whitman.

Although many teachers and parents realize "nobody's perfect", they still may expect perfection. This excellent book helps children, ages 5 to 9 deal with the reality of imperfect behavior.

Chapter 12

Child-Focused Parent Groups

This chapter takes parent involvement in the counseling process a step further with the discussion of parent groups. Topics included in this chapter are: the value of parent groups; development of the group; the operation, format, and content of the group; and combining children and parents in groups. The child-focused parent group is presented in this chapter as another collaborative strategy designed to help, support, and encourage parents in improving and strengthening their relationships with their children.

Learning Objectives

Upon completing this chapter, you will be able to:

1. Define and discuss the value of parent groups.

2. Identify the keys to forming a successful group.

3. Describe the operational, format, content, and evaluation components of the parent group.

4. Define and discuss the value of the parent-child group.

5. Describe the structure, operation, content, and evaluation related to the parent-child group.

Review Exercises

1. What is a parent group? What is the value of such a group to the participating parents, to their children, and to the counselor?

2. Describe the historical beginnings of the concept of the parent group. List and describe the five models of parent groups according to approach and orientation.

3. What is the common thread or common goal that characterizes these groups?

4. As part of involving parents as partners in planning the group, what five things will the counselor need to do?

5. What is group structure? What parents "types" should be represented in the group?

6. Contrast a balanced and an imbalanced parent group.

7. What preparations are necessary in forming a group related to invitation and welcome, time and date parameters, and number of participants?

8. What problems related to question 7 can be anticipated? How can they be resolved?

9. What are the four basic principles of behavior (Adlerian assumptions), and how are these utilized in the parent group?

10. List the three basic ground rules needed to build trust in the group, to protect the parents in the group as well as guide the counselor in facilitating the group.

11. What are "group goals"? How are they determined?

12. What are five advantages of the small-group format?

13. What are the five ways by which parents are assisted to communicate in the group using hypothetical family situations?

14. Describe the techniques that can be used in parent groups including hypothetical situations, group discussion, and role play.

15. Why is follow-up of individuals who drop out of the group so important?

16. What are some methods that can be used for evaluating group effectiveness?

17. List four discussion topics that may be helpful to groups that are just getting started.

18. Parent groups can be developmental, preventive, or remedial in focus. Define these terms.

19. What is a parent-child group? How and why is it formed?

20. List the keys to a successful parent-child group.

Awareness Exercises

1. What are your feelings about parent groups and parent-child groups? Do you think they are a "good thing?" Would you want to be involved in such groups? Do you think you would feel comfortable being a facilitator?

2. Which of the five types of group approaches (i.e., Adlerian, humanistic, behavioral, structured, and unstructured support groups) do you feel most attracted to? Why?

3. A grandmother's statement is quoted in the section entitled "Definition and Value of Parent Groups." Do you agree or disagree with this statement? Do you find that sharing your feelings "lightens your load"? Why or why not?

4. As the counselor/facilitator of the parent group, do you think it would be most advantageous in fulfilling your role as counselor if you have children of your own or do not have children? Is parenthood irrelevant to your success as a parent-group facilitator? Please choose a position, elaborate, and support your answer.

5. Are there some persons with a particular ethnic, racial, economic, religious or political background with whom you might find it difficult to be with and relate to in a parent group? Why? Why not?

6. Can you think of some hypothetical situations useful for group discussions that are not included in the text? Write down some of your ideas for future reference and/or class discussion.

7. How comfortable do you think you would be facilitating a parent-child group? Why? Why not?

8. Read the evaluative comments that parents and children wrote regarding the parent-child group experience. Do you think these are useful things to have learned? Comment on each.

Practical Applications

Parent Groups

Open-ended hypothetical family situations can be used to open parent group discussions. The following are a few examples of problems that commonly occur during childhood. Some are developmental concerns that are common to all children, and others reflect specific problems that are experienced by a few. These hypothetical family situations were taken from the actual experience of parents in the group. It is recommended that the reader develop his or her own situations based on the concerns of current group members. As trust and cohesion develop, the group discussion generally focuses on the parents' personal concerns for their children.

"Don't Suck Your Thumb!"

Tyrone Tyler sucks his thumb. This habit upsets and worries his parents a great deal. When Tyrone sucks his thumb in the presence of company, his mother pulls the thumb from his mouth and says sharply, "Don't suck your thumb!" or " Look at 'baby' suck his thumb!" After a while, Tyrone puts his thumb right back into his mouth. Both of his parents have tried taping his thumb, coloring it with chili powder, and putting a sock on it. All of these things do not help. As a matter of fact, Tyrone sucks his thumb now more than ever.

1. Discuss some of the possible reasons for Tyrone's thumb sucking.

_____

2. Give your ideas about the methods that Tyrone's parents are using to change his thumb-sucking habit and discuss why you think they are ineffective. What are your ideas for helping Tyrone quit?

_____

"You're Going to Get Your Mouth Washed Out with Soap!"

Chang, age 5, swears at home and at school. Chang's father, upset with his swearing, says, "Get into the bathroom. You're going to get your mouth washed out with soap!"

1. How do you think children learn to swear?

_____

_____

2. What benefit, if any , do youngsters get from using profanity?

_____

_____

3. What else could Chang's father do to teach him not to swear?

_____

_____

_____

"What Would You Do About Hamad?"

It is a family rule at the Smith house that the children must walk home directly after school. Young Hamad, age 9, has been coming home later and later each day. Last Tuesday it was 5:00 p.m. before Hamad got home.

1. If you were Hamad's parent(s), how would you have handled the situation?

_____

_____

"Boys Will Be Boys"

Sam Malone's father has always looked upon his son's mischievousness with a "boys will be boys" attitude. He has just been informed by the school principal that Sam threw a rock in the school window.

1. How do you think Mr. Malone will react?

_____

_____

2. If you were Sam's father, what would you do?

_____

_____

"There's a Monster Under My Bed"

Jack is 6 years old and doesn't want to go to bed at night. He tells his mother that there is "a monster under my bed." She tries to talk him out of being afraid by saying "Don't be silly, there are no such things as monsters!" His father tells him there is nothing to fear and ridicules him by saying "Don't be such a big baby!" Jack's parents leave the light on but this doesn't help. On some occasions, especially during thunderstorms, Jack asks to sleep with his parents.

1. How you would handle this situation if you were Jack's parents?

_____

_____

"Speeding Toward Destruction"

Alex is 14 and is hooked on methamphetamine, a stimulant known as "speed". At first he took the pills to feel good about himself, but now he finds that he needs more and more of them to get the same effect. He is frightened by the crazy things that he has been doing lately. His agitation and anxiety have given way to panic and he doesn't know what to do.

His allowance provided him with the pills until his mother, angry with him for his poor school grades, discontinued it. Now he has been stealing money from her purse and from the other kids at school. He has been in trouble with the law several times, but his mother, who has custody of him and his brother, has always believed his excuses and has defended him. His father, who has since remarried, wants him to face the consequences of his actions.

1. What might be some reasons why kids, like Alex, experiment with and get hooked on drugs?

_____

_____

2. As a parent, how would you help him or her?

_____

_____

3. Pretend that you are Alex and tell another parent at your table that you are hooked on drugs. How would you react if your child were telling you this and asked for help?

_____

_____

Parent-Child Groups

Hypothetical family situations that are common to both children and their parents can be used to start the parent-child discussion. These situations help to facilitate communication between parents and children. After the group develops trust and cohesion, discussion often centers around the participants' own home and family problems. The following are examples of situations that occur in the lives of today's children.

"Home Alone"

Shalene and Janui are home alone after school while their mother works until 5:00 p.m. They always have a snack, watch, television or play with their toys. One day while they were watching TV, they heard a knock at the door. They peeked through the window and saw a person whom they didn't recognize.

1. What should Shalene and Janui do? Should they open the door?

_____

_____

2. What instructions do you think their mother left for them?

_____

_____

"Promise You Won't Tell"

One day when they were playing, Dylan told his sister, Heather, a secret that she promised not to reveal to anyone. Dylan confessed that he had accidently broken his mother's antique vase but that she didn't know it yet. He replaced the large chip that fell out and turned the vase around so his mother wouldn't notice. About a week later their mother discovered the broken vase and asked if anyone knew what had happened to it.

1. What do you think Heather should do? If she breaks her promise, Dylan will get punished. If she doesn't tell, she will have to lie to her mother.

_____

_____

_____

What would you do in a similar situation?

_____

_____

_____

Media Suggestions

Books

Boyd-Franklin, N. (1989). *Black Families in Therapy.* New York: Guilford Press.

Family empowerment is the theme of this therapeutic guide. It stresses the importance of sensitivity to the ethnic and cultural heritage of families who are seeking help.

Calderone, M.S. (1989). *Family Book About Sexuality.* New York: Harper & Row.

This is a classic, comprehensive guide to sexuality. It offers a compendium of facts and issues, sensitively addressed, including the development of sexuality through life, reproduction, family planning, sexually transmitted diseases, drugs and sex, abortion, homosexuality and other aspects of human sexual life.

Cole, J. (1988). *Asking About Sex and Growing Up.* New York: Morrow Junior Books.

This question and answer book for preteens presents a healthy attitude toward sex and growing up-- one that children need to hear while they are still young. It has simple pictures and clearly worded text. Highly recommended.

Hatfield, A.B. (1990). *Families of the Mentally Ill: Meeting the Challenges.* New York: Guilford Press.

Mental illness has hidden victims. Often, it's the families of the mentally ill who must face community stigma and ignorance. This book is about the family advocacy movement and the empowering effect it has had on the mental health establishment. A must!

Johnson, J. (1994). *Hidden Victims: An Eight-Stage Healing Process for Families and Friends of the Mentally Ill.* Minneapolis, MN: PEMA Publications.

This book offers practical and realistic help for the "hidden victims" of mental illness. The author urges family members to accept mental illness as they would accept any chronic illness, to learn to cope with fear and guilt and to limit the disruptive effects on the family.

Nichols, M. P. (1993). *Power of the Family.* Klamath Falls, OR: Gardner Press.

A family therapist's guide to how families work and how they get stuck. This book offers suggestions on how to deal with a number of family problems including sibling rivalry and adolescent drug use.

Schwebel, A. (1989). *Guide to a Happier Family: Overcoming the Anger, Frustration and Boredom that Destroy Family Life.* New York: J.P. Tarcher.

Written by a family of therapists, this book offers an antidote to the anger, frustration, and boredom that threaten to destroy almost all families at some time. Discussion revolves around overcoming family problems and finding ways to enhance the love, caring, and intimacy we all seek.

Solomon, C. (1989). *The Parent/Child Manual on Latchkey Kids.* New York: Tor Books.

Read this book aloud together. It has cartoons and lots of good advice about how to be happy and safe alone at home.

Videos

Can We Talk? FH: Films for the Humanities and Sciences, P.O. Box 2053, Princeton, NJ 08543-2053.

This video features a family communications skills test in game-show format, featuring vignettes by the *Cosby Show* and *Family Ties* kids. Expert commentators discuss resolutions. (52 minutes, color).

Family Affair: Educating Today's Parents. FH: Films for the Humanities and Sciences, P.O. Box 2053, Princeton, NJ 08543-2053.

This video explores the techniques that can lead to "good" parenting and illustrates what works and what doesn't. It focuses on how "parent groups" provide learning and support, explores strategies for raising a family, and discusses where and how to obtain information that can assist parents. (24 minutes, color).

Psychology of Parenting. FH: Films for the Humanities and Sciences, P.O. Box 2053, Princeton, NJ 08543-2053.

The viewer has an opportunity to visit a workshop and listen to parents as they share the positive and the negative aspects of child rearing. This film offers suggestions for better communication with teenagers.

The Latino Family FH: Films for the Humanities and Sciences, P.O. Box 2053, Princeton, NJ 08543-2053.

This presentation highlights the changes and the endurance of traditional Latino families. In following three generations of one Mexican-American family, it traces the patterns of migration and cultural change. It shows how the traditional roles of the Latino elderly are being altered by their families' needs and how family traditions can still be celebrated. (28 minutes, color)